A
GOOD WORD
for a
BETTER LIFE

A COMPILATION OF DAILY MEDITATIONS

BISHOP HORACE SHEFFIELD

OSP Publishing

About The Author
Rev. Horace L. Sheffield, Ill.

The Reverend Horace L. Sheffield, III, was born in Detroit, Michigan during the midst of the Civil Rights and Labor Movements to Horace L., Jr., and Mary Sheffield. Through the work and legacy of his father, Horace L. Sheffield, Jr., who was the vice president of the Negro American Labor Council (NALC) under A. Philip Randolph, it's founder and president, Rev. Sheffield, III, was providentially exposed to various enduring models of "servant leadership" and "prophetic societal challenge."

Called to preached in June, 1965 at eleven years of age, while listening to the preaching of Dr. Martin L. King, Jr., who was in Detroit at the invitation of his father to raise money for the Lowndes County Movement, Rev. Horace L. Sheffield, III, was licensed to preach on October 18, 1978 at the First Baptist Institutional Church of Detroit, Michigan and was subsequently ordained there by his spiritual father and ministry mentor, the Reverend Dr. Howard B. M. Fauntroy, Jr.

In addition to writing plays, Rev. Sheffield has also published articles and other materials in the Michigan Chronicle, the Detroit News, the Michigan Front Page, the African American Parent Magazine, and a variety of other periodicals, television and radio programming, as well as numerous newsletters and community circulars.

Presently, Rev. Horace L. Sheffield, III, is the pastor of Detroit's New Destiny Baptist Church, known for *"Transforming Communities*

By Changing Lives," where, under his leadership, the congregation successfully completed the construction of a new edifice. In addition to his congregational duties and pastoral work, Rev. Sheffield, is also the executive director of the Detroit Association of Black Organizations (dabo) where he established and administers their Detroit Cares Alternative High School, an alternative education high school, Project Self-Sufficiency, a program providing GED instruction and job training for youth, and manages all of the other various social and economic programs of the agency.

Rev. Sheffield also served on the staff of Detroit's Mayor Dennis W. Archer, was a former Board Member of St. John NorthEast Community Hospital, is president of the Michigan Chapter of the National Action Network (NAN), is chairperson of the Detroit Ecumenical Ministers Alliance, is a national board member of the Black Leadership Commission on AIDs, is a national board member of the National Cares Movement under the leadership of Susan Taylor, and is a life member of the NAACP. Rev. Sheffield hosts his own weekly radio show known as "On The Line," which formerly aired every Saturday on WCHB AM 1200, and now airs every Friday from 2-3:30 PM on AM 910 the Word Radio Network. Rev. Sheffield is also seen in over 200 million homes around the world on his religious broadcast which airs twice a week on the WORD Television Network.

Rev. Sheffield has two children, Horace Lindsey Sheffield, IV, a musical producer, and Minister Mary Christine Sheffield, an elected member of the Detroit City Council. Rev. Sheffield lives by the motto and credo that once served as his father's.

"All the world is my homeland, and all of its people with their many tongues and many religions are my brethren. And the fight for full justice and freedom for all of them is my religion, and my indomitable strength in this flows from my unshakable belief that this is God's will!"

Rev. Sheffield, when asked how he would like to have his life best described has stated, "When fate shall capture this mortal flesh and my soul shall soar to reap its imperishable reward on distant shore may it be said by those who knew Horace L. Sheffield, III, best that '*he loved God and people and sought to love and to serve both.*"

Table of Contents

Introduction

Over the last thirty some odd years of pastoring there has been one common occurrence in each of the churches I have pastored--words that people have said or read that have impacted and impaired both their walk with the Lord and service to His church. Consequently, I have developed a discipline of both reading daily devotionals and meditations for myself and of trying to provide the same for the people I have been blessed to pastor. It is my hope that this treatise will so inspire you to find your own fountain and to drink from it each and every day.

This book represents some of those "Words from the Pastor" that I have been blessed to write during my past tenure as senior pastor of the New Galilee Missionary Baptist Church and during my current term with the New Destiny Christian Fellowship, both of Detroit, Michigan. While many of these meditations were written while at these two churches much of the insight contained within them was also gleaned from my work at New Light Baptist (Detroit) and from my pastorates at Renaissance Christian Church and Bethel United Methodist Church in Brooklyn, New York.

I have been so blessed to not only have words to encourage me but also a "cloud of witnesses" who spoke life and power into my life. I want to thank and honor Mrs. Lula Davis, my first grade homeroom teacher at Roosevelt Elementary, who told me at six that I had a brilliant mind; Mr. William Jackson, my history teacher at Cass Tech and my true life mentor, who after my mother's tragic death, would not let me die as well; Sister Lola Mack who brought me to First Baptist Institutional and introduced me to my father in the gospel, Dr. Howard B. M. Fauntroy, Jr.; Dr. Howard Fauntroy, who sensed my call, and consequently launched my ministry; Sis. Lula Mae Badgett who tragically lost her son, the same age as me, my first week of pastoring Bethel and became my spiritual mother for all eternity; Albert Lyons who was so touched by my ministry in Brooklyn that he became the greatest evangelist I ever met; Dr. Delton Fernander, a younger man than I, yet my pastor and my earthly guide; Prophetess Shameka Morley who helps me see what my corrected and revised vision fails to notice; and, to my entire New Destiny Christian Fellowship that has proven to me that a church can love someone back to life.

Finally, I dedicate this book to my grandparents, Horace and Georgia Sheffield, and to my parents Horace and Mary Sheffield who encompassed my sisters and I with so much love and devotion that it was hard to imagine that heaven could be any better; to my two loving sisters who are to me what Martha and Mary were to Jesus; to my wonderful children: Horace Lindsey Sheffield, IV, who promises to be a person of great legacy and destiny, and Mary Christine Sheffield, who has taken on my family passion for fighting for the defenseless; and, and finally for Esha Price, who is becoming something and someone to me that no one has ever been. I live everyday for those I love, for my family, and especially for my children.

CHAPTER 1

"It's Time To Choose"

(Joshua 24:15)

WE ALL HAVE character flaws that can coerce our choices and our conduct to comply and to bow to them.

Some of these character flaws were coerced by what we were forced to be exposed to early in life, some are learned responses, some are acquired appetites, and some of them really reflect our preferences.

Nonetheless, these flaws will always manifest themselves unless we have freed ourselves from them. And when they do they compel us to be and to do things that do not resemble the person we present, nor the one we are trying to be, or result in our best interest.

And this contest between our wills and our inscribed and coerced habits, carefully camouflaged yet detectible, forces others to both witness it and suffer from it. Too many times those who are attached to these recklessly driven people suffer even more because the person gripped by such harmful and hurtful compulsions is unable to share the truth about the same with their loved ones. Therefore, we are ill affected by the choices of others.

Whether the person gripped by such affliction desires to, a choice still has to be made. The person afflicted must decide whether what can be, and what they now have is more attractive and worth more than what they've been governed by in the past and are still compelled by in the present.

No choice sometimes compels others to make a choice that they would not like to make, but they have no other options because they've been given no choice.

It's time to choose. And know this: that all choices and non-choices have consequences.

CHAPTER 2

What is Leadership?

SEVERAL YEARS AGO, while working for Mayor Archer, I attended a leadership seminar. Some of the information I received there still remains with me to this day. While this seminar took place in a secular setting, and not in a church, it still had some spiritual significance. I just thought that I would share a few of the main points I learned then about **"WHAT LEADERSHIP IS,"** and then I will close with a particularly pertinent quote from *GOETHE* that I hope you will incorporate into your being and doing here at New Destiny as I am endeavoring to do as well.

LEADERSHIP IS

Who you are when no one is looking!

LEADERSHIP IS

Doing whatever it takes to make something happens - even if you do it alone!

LEADERSHIP IS

Making adversity your ally!

LEADERSHIP IS

Having and maintaining an irrational sense of hope!

LEADERSHIP IS
>Knowing that no one has to lose for you to win!

LEADERSHIP IS
>Aligning your daily efforts with your distant dreams!

LEADERSHIP IS
>Knowing that your life has a purpose beyond the path where it now leads!

And now for a particularly pertinent quote from Goethe, and one from me, which as I have already said - that daily I try to abide by more and more.

"God called me to build the Kingdom, not to crush pebbles." **(Rev. Horace L. Sheffield, III, Pastor, New Destiny)**

CHAPTER 3

Tough Talk?

"OBEY THEM THAT have rule over you, and submit yourselves..." These are tough words, but they are not mine. They are God's. Somewhere along the road, we have forgotten, in our pursuit of church work that God does have a prescribed order and a fixed plan regarding the governance of His Church, and the role that His called leadership is to exercise within it. We have become so accustomed to exercising our wills, promoting our approaches, and voicing our opinions that we often overlook and ignore God's instruction about what order he has established for His church, and how it should be respected, understood, and followed.

Tough talk, though true talk, is the fact that even in the Baptist church, notwithstanding the notion or the governing principle that the *"congregation's voice is final in all matters,"* God intended and still requires that the elder, overseer, or pastor to be the one who leads. Nowhere in the Bible does God have more than one leader on point or in authority at one time. Choose who you will—Moses, David, James, or Peter--there is never a time in the Bible where there is more than one godly appointed and anointed leader through whom God works His Will, and the people are expected to follow. **Tough Talk - God only has one leader at one time.**

Oh, but those of you who always find a way to reject leadership will say: "But what about God, Jesus and the Holy Spirit? They all share leadership. Wrong, while on earth Jesus was in charge, "all authority in heaven and earth" (remember Jesus saying this), and while in heaven and after Jesus' return, the three are one, and only one is in charge. Now, nobody is arguing for a pastoral dictatorship - just for us to honor the WORD, and having us - even me - to OBEY - follow-them that have rule over you [us]. Tough Talk - God will move in our midst when we line up with Him, and line up with the leader *He* has placed here as pastor and given authority to.

"Obey them that have rule over you, and submit yourselves...for they must give an account." Obey. That's the word. People in church often act like children who want to challenge their parent's authority. In the church, God has placed pastors as the leaders of the church. And in the Baptist church the necessary checks and balances on that authority come from the congregation, who, when they meet decide, based on the Bible and having heard from God, not based on how they feel, how it will affect them, or on whether they like what the pastor is doing, if in fact what is proposed is truly of God *(decide by try the Spirit or judging the fruit)*.

Obey. Submit. Follow. This is what God has commanded us to do by way of our pastors, not challenge, condemn, or be pulled in different directions. Here is some tough talk, if God wanted you to be the leader, He would have called you to be the pastor - or found you a church of your own to pastor.

CHAPTER 4

"As Simple As Science - No Spiritual Shortcuts"

"But seek ye FIRST the kingdom of God, and his righteousness; and all these things shall be added unto you" (Matthew 6:33).

AFTER MANY YEARS in the ministry I have observed this one simple truth: if there was a way for people to gain from God the goods without having to live any differently, change anything, or have to be responsible for rendering any sort of service to God or the church--they would. We live in an era in which prophets, priests, popular personalities, and even the church regularly sells the saints "spiritual shortcuts" - that is, a way to get God to do something for them without them having to do much, or, if possible, nothing at all.

Well, I write today to tell you that this extracting from the eternal without any sense of obligation, commitment, or the notion that nothing is expected from us - first or in return- is **FALSE**. Here's what I believe, and you can quote me, *"If we want God to do something supernatural for US - then we have to do something simple for HIM - Like Obey Him, Live for Him, and Serve Him."* There is no place in sacred scripture, with the exception of salvation, in which we are required to do nothing to receive something. We have to ask before we can receive, knock before the door is opened, and even call before we are answered. Why then, if this is true, do we expect God to lavish a luxurious lifestyle upon us, provide us with perpetual prosperity, pay our mortgages and car notes, bless us in bankruptcy, and grant us every request we make without something he receives from us first or in exchange for what he bestows upon us?

To the contrary, God does require us to give him our trust first, to put him first, and to obey him first before we can access his inexhaustible supply. This notion of supply, of provision, and of the nature and quality of our relationship with God is as simple as science, and cannot and will not be gained through spiritual shortcuts. The truth of this tale is in the text above. If you want all to be added unto you--peace of mind, prosperity, joy, and any other imaginable benefit from God--so much so that there is not enough room for you to receive it ALL - **PUT GOD FIRST**. And I am a living witness, that if this is done God becomes first and last in your life. Then everything else between his being first and last will be bountiful, blessed, and non-intermittent.

CHAPTER 5

"Knowing Our End Helps Us Now!"

"Lord, make me to know my end, and the measure of my days, what it is, that I may know how frail I am" (Psalm 39:4).

It was reported that an unnamed expert on learning once said that "time teaches all things to he who lives forever, but none of us have the luxury of eternity." Beloved, if it is one thing that I have learned it is how swiftly our lives come and how quickly they come to a close. There is no excess of time. All we have, in terms of time on this earth, is that the time God has allotted us is certain, fixed.

This recognition of the limitedness of our lives is expressed by David in this Psalm. "Lord, help me to know my end that I begin to live to be prepared now as if the end were near." Too many of us procrastinate and live as if we always have tomorrow and therefore leave undone matters that we should rectify before we die. We consume ourselves with pleasures, appetites, and priorities that simply ignore the fact that at any instant we may well have to stand before God and give an account for every self-centered second, every messed up minute, every hurtful hour, every decadent day, and every unyielding hour.

I don't know about you - but as I approach fifty years of age I have begun to take stock of time, both the time already spent and hopefully what is left. I have in essence begun to "measure" my days. I have measured how many days were spent for God and how many were spent on me. How many days did I do wrong, and how many days did I do right? That is to say, I have honestly assessed how I have lived those years already spent and then asked God for enough time left to allow my good days to outweigh my bad days, and to at least balance my account.

How about You? Have you come to a point in which you recognize that the time you have left may be less than the time you've already had? Or, have you noticed that you are no longer a child, a teenager, or even a young adult and yet your withdrawals from the bank of time are leaving you fewer days left? Then meditate on this Psalm and decide, beginning this second, to live each day as if it were your last, and to know that how you live may influence how long you live.

CHAPTER 6

"Hearing God!"

"...and the sheep follow him; for they know his
voice" **(Romans 2:1, KJV).**

OF ALL THE spiritual disciplines that I need to employ to succeed by daily saintly sojourn in this wicked and seductive world below, hearing God is more important and valuable than all. Yet, even though hearing from God is a priority in terms of avoiding pitfalls, overcoming obstacles, and eliminating evil entanglements, it remains a difficult and rarely practiced discipline. We listen to ourselves more than we do God and wonder why we have what we have, are what we are, and are headed where we are headed.

What makes hearing from God, and knowing His voice so difficult? First, we cannot hear God because we don't speak His language. Too many of us prefer for someone else to decipher, discern, and to determine what God is saying to us, about us, and about what to do and where we should be. We rely on others because we have not, will not, and do not study God's Word. **God's Word is God's Voice.** When Jesus spoke in this passage - God's people knew his voice, and he could say they did because they had studied God's Word, listened to the prophets, and had sat under teachers to receive instruction. God, when he spoke, used His learned word as the language by which he communicated with His people.

Today, we are biblically illiterate and therefore spiritually ignorant when it comes to distinguishing God's voice from ours, from the world, from others, from Satan, and even from the church. If there is any pursuit that is a priority in our spiritual quest and ecclesiastical engagements it is to hear God's voice. For in his voice is understanding, direction, instruction and guidance, deliverance, healing, prosperity, renewal, without which we are bound to fall, falter, and follow someone and something other than Jesus.

As I come to a close let me answer the question that still lingers, *"how do we know that it is God's voice?"* First, to hear God we must separate ourselves and find a quiet place. Secondly, we can tell God's voice by both the **TONE** and the **CONTENT**, that is, how it is spoken and what is said. God's voice is not of a roaring lion - but a small still voice. And he will never speak anything contrary to his nature, his will, and his purpose as has already been revealed in His Word, the Bible.

Finally, let me just state that the best life, and the most measured life, comes not from listening to self or to others but in having your conversations with God and then obeying what you were told. Amen.

CHAPTER **7**

"My Non-Negotiable?"

I GREW UP in a union home. My father spent most of his life both working to gain the union's acceptance by private enterprise, as well as working to get unions, once they were recognized, to accept the overall plight of the Negro in American society and within their unions as non-marginalized members. For my father, the fate and condition of black workers within unions and within this nation was a nonnegotiable item in exchange for his support of the unions.

Paul, in I Corinthians 2:2, approaches his connectedness to the church, and his interpersonal interaction with the saints, with a comparable sense of having some non-negotiable. In other words, regardless of what the issues were in the church, who was at odds with who, what all could not agree on, and even the personal animosity that others in the church had toward him, his non-negotiable was that he was determined - while in church - and while around others in the fellowship - *"not to know anything....save Jesus Christ, and him crucified."* Paul's non-negotiable, while in church meetings, board meetings, choir rehearsals, and when the church gathered to worship was not to experience (or to know, Epignosis in the Greek) anything except Jesus and Him crucified, or that is, God and His Power.

Beloved, believe it or not, we decide what we experience when we come to church, what we contribute while here, and what we take with us when we leave. And I am a firm believer, and have been convicted by Christ about this, that what I experience in church has more to do with me, my frame of mind, what I seek in the service, than it has to do with anybody or anything else. Seeing, talking to, fellowshipping with, and hearing from Jesus when I am in church has become and is my non-negotiable. Therefore, what Jesus does when I am here speaks louder than anything anyone else says, does, is thinking of me, or didn't do. **I am here for Him.** And the more I experience Him, then the more what I experience between you and me becomes more Christ-like.

Will you today, like Paul, decide to have a non-negotiable about your church life? Will the most important consideration about church for you become experiencing Jesus and His Power? That's why I am here today and my non-negotiable is *now*: To place myself in fellowship with Him and not with unbelievers; To acquaint myself with his authority and not the opinions of others; To immerse myself in His Presence and not the sub-surface scenarios that obscure my view of Him. I want to simply learn more of Him and to better *do* His Will.

My non-negotiable is to see Jesus, the man who bled and died for me, and to, by fellowshipping with Him and the saints, incorporate into my life the same power that raised Jesus from the dead.

CHAPTER 8

"GOOD GOD!"

"O Give thanks unto the Lord; for he is good....."
(Psalm 136:1, KJV)

GOOD GOD. I have often said about this phrase, as far back as my first pastorate in Brooklyn, New York, that when James Brown, the legendary soul singer, used this expression he had something else in mind than I do. When James Brown would exclaim "good god" it was his way of "affirming his funkiness" on stage. However, when I say "GOOD GOD" it is my way of "describing God's attributes" in the presence of God's people.

Make no mistake about it, **"God is a GOOD GOD."** God is a good God because he is so regardless of us. What I mean is that God's goodness is independent of our affirmation, recognition, and our acknowledgment. God does need us to affirm that He is good; the "rocks" are prepared to tell that story. God does not need us to recognize that He is good for the heavens cannot wait to "declare His glory." And God does not need us to acknowledge His goodness for each and every day that this earth continues to exist, and the oceans remain secure, it is a testimony to who God is and what he does.

Notice that the Psalmist also attests to the independent goodness of God when he states "for he is good." The very nature of God is goodness. A nature and a goodness that never ceases, is never altered, and is never exhausted. To be sure, we have trouble relating to God as a good God who remains so even when responding to us, his own, because we are disobedient, disrespectful, and decadent. You see we change, we go back and forth, and our godliness changes based on how we feel on any given day. But God is different. He isn't one way one day and another way on a different day, God stays the *same* - GOOD!

GOOD GOD. This year at Thanksgiving I will pause to praise the God of my youth, the God of my wilderness, and the God of my salvation. My God is a Good God. God is a GOOD GOD because He protects me, He provides for me, He understands me, He feeds me, He corrects me, He speaks to me, He makes my enemies my footstool, He hides me in His secret place, He washes me, He forgives me, He blots out my transgressions, He chastises me, He redeems me, He leads me, He encourages me, He comforts me, He makes up for things that I have lost (my mother, my father, etc.), He delivers me from my own devices, He's a very present help in time of trouble, and every day He **IS MORE** to **ME** than **He** has **ALREADY BEEN**. *My God is a GOOD GOD.* **How about yours?**

CHAPTER 9

"Are You A Christian Criminal?"

IN MALACHI, THE prophet speaking for God clearly identifies the withholding of the Lord's money, by those who have claimed Him as their own, in the form of tithes and offerings as a *crime* - **Robbery!** Having recently reflected on the record of our members giving, particularly those in leadership, and others who regularly and openly express their public praise of God in this church, I have come to the conclusion that among us exist some **"Christian Criminals."** That is to say, that there are those among us who simply **do not trust God**--or must feel that they are exempt from **God's Proscription** even though they regularly rely upon **His Provision.**

This issue of **"robbing God"** or of there being **"Christian Criminals"** in the church is one that bothers me deeply. Why? Because God says in his Word that those who are guilty are *cursed*. And if they are cursed, and they are in the leadership and doing ministry in this church - it naturally follows then that their condition would result in the same being true for our church - *cursed*.

We no longer have to figure out how to improve our church's finances, it is quite clear. Trust and Obey God, and **Just Tithe**. If not, then you simply **do not trust God**, and if you do not trust God in your own life--you certainly cannot trust God in the life of the church.

Consequently, you should step down until such time as you can lead by example, live by the Word, and no longer exempt yourself from what God has required of *all* - that you do not do - yet expect and ask others to.

And if you do not believe that you are a **"Christian Criminal"** read it for yourself: *Malachi 3:8, "Will a man ROB God? Yet ye have robbed me. But ye say, Wherein have we robbed thee? In tithes and offerings..."* And what does the Word say about those Christian Criminals who do not do this, *"Ye are CURSED with a curse: for ye have robbed ME..."* (Malachi 3:9).

Let me remind you that Paul says in I Corinthians 5 that a "little yeast leaveneth the whole loaf." **What you do or do not do affects the Whole Body**. We will never prosper as a church if those in the boardroom, pulpit, singing solos, teaching Sunday school, or who present themselves in any position of leadership in this church fail to trust God enough to **TITHE**. Let me remind you that **LEADERSHIP IS** - who you are when no one is looking! And that, **LEADERSHIP IS** - doing whatever it takes to make something happen - even if you do it alone!

In closing, as we prepare budgets, raise money for the anniversary, and discuss the church's financial condition, also remember what Goethe said, *"The things which matter MOST must never be at the mercy of the things which matter LEAST."* What matters most is that **TITHING COMES FIRST.**

CHAPTER 10

"Let the Record Reflect"

"Be ye Holy; for I am Holy (I Peter 1:16)

LET THE RECORD reflect, that unlike some ministers-politicians and other religious leaders in secular circles, that I do not support, endorse, or approve of gay marriages.

Let the record reflect, that having attended a seminary in the late 1970s and early 1980s that was almost defined by its liberalism, especially how eagerly both the student body and faculty embraced homosexuality, I have long had to wrestle with this moral dilemma of loving the person yet rejecting the sin. One's human sexuality *is* a personal choice - and one that to some degree is governed by civil society, through the granting of licenses, divorces, etc., but ultimately and absolutely marriage is governed by God. And no matter what man--with whatever sexual orientation they possess may suggest, God's law as it relates to the opposite sex – God-ordained Holy Matrimony is **INVIOLABLE** by the State of California and even the United States Supreme Court. God is not for **SAME SEX MARRIAGES.**

Let the record reflect - God does not support gay marriages, and God does not approve of homosexuality. Let the record reflect that I am concerned with the potential mainstreaming of morally socially deviant behavior. By allowing same sex marriages in a country that even all our secular themes suggests, (like the national anthem, America the Beautiful, etc.), that God was responsible for this land through His Grace--dishonors and disrespects the very God we claim to be the backbone and guiding force of our nation.

Now, let the record also reflect that while I do not endorse same sex marriages for moral reasons, and based on Christian ethics, I also do so out of concern for the social damage that is being done to our young people as a result of the open acceptance of this un-Christian lifestyle. The consequences of this growing gay culture are staggering. Right here in the city of Detroit our public schools are besieged with young women–and a growing expression of lesbianism that at times has threatened public safety in our public schools. Well, when such suggestions of acceptability of these lifestyles are so socially apparent politically, and even within our churches, what is there then left to provide Christian moral influence to our children and to this world that such sinful indulgence is not okay–even if the government of San Francisco says it is.

Let the record reflect I am not anti-gay, just anti-sin: heterosexual and homosexual sin.And like me, hopefully you see both as the same and are fleeing both.

CHAPTER 11

Why Do I Need
To Come To Church?

I ENCOUNTER SO many people who always ask this somewhat simi-lar question, **"If I read my Bible at home, pray every day, and try my best to live a good Christian life, do I really need to come to church on Sunday morning"?**

Unfortunately for those of us who have convinced ourselves otherwise, who like to use Sunday as a leisure take-care-of-our-own-business day, and who like to sleep late on Sunday, the unavoidable and direct answer to that question is a resounding - **YES.** There is no question that it is vitally important for us to come to church *every* Sunday, and in fact, for us to even endeavor to form the habit of coming to New Destiny *every* Sunday.

It makes no difference if my preaching is poor and what I say bores you to death. It doesn't really matter if your brother or sister in the Lord, sitting beside you or in the next pew, is an obvious hypocrite who struts on Sunday and crawls on Monday, or who prays fervently in church and yet mistreats his fellow man during the week. And it doesn't even matter if the worship service, the choir, or the preaching drags on to the point that you feel irritated and bothered as opposed to being warmed with a radiant glow from above.

The main objective and the primary reason we participate in worship and we come to church is worship. Like our private prayers, it is a ***"time-tested and dependable means of drawing nigh unto God."***

If you come to New Destiny anxiously expecting to meet the Lord here, you will not leave disappointed. However, if you come so closed that you refuse to let anyone or anything move you or fellowship with you, you will leave here worse off than when you came.

Jesus can and will speak to you through our coming together, through divine worship, through the most boring sermon, through the choir that can't seem to carry a note, and through the soloist who you wonder why anyone would let them sing - if, ***if you*** are sincerely seeking and praying to hear His Voice.

So I ask you, as pastor, to make a more meaningful commitment and a more serious effort to be faithful in your attendance of Divine worship and to come prayerfully each and every Sunday seeking to hear His Voice. If you come he'll be here!

CHAPTER 12

"A PAUSE for the CAUSE"

"And Jesus STOOD STILL, and commanded him
to be called. And they called the blind man, saying
unto him, Be of good comfort, rise; he calleth thee"
(Mark 10:49).

AND JESUS **STOOD STILL**. Now, if you were obedient and took time last week to come to the pastor's Bible study you would know how significant it is that Jesus **STOOD STILL**. If I can - let me first say that we have been taught - and exhorted recently - that the way to get Jesus' attention is through *praise*. However, this text teaches us that a man who first acknowledged Jesus for who he actually was, and then asked for mercy –(not means) got Jesus' undivided attention.

Here is this blind man begging by the side of the road. And here comes Jesus, with his disciples who he had to leave behind before they would follow him on the way to his death, not so consumed with his own personal problems and troubling circumstances that he could not see and hear the needs of others. And so even though Jesus is pressing his way to die, he pauses for the cause, the cause of blessing a blind beggar who had enough and could hear enough to know that Jesus was the Son of David, or the long-awaited Savior.

And this man, blind Bartimaeus, hearing Jesus - refused to be hushed as he both acknowledged His King and sought Mercy all at once. The power of this moment, someone who was an outsider, someone who was blind and who did not have the advantage of seeing Jesus feed the 5000, walk on water, raise the dead, and yet he knew exactly who Jesus was–and did not seek means (sight, money, etc.) but rather simply sought mercy.

And Jesus **STOOD STILL**. I believe he stood still because at least he had encountered someone who had it right. Someone who did not need to be told who Jesus was and who was not seeking to exploit who he was for a personal favor. Blind Bartimaeus praised Jesus as Savior and simply asked for mercy. And this recognition of Christ and need for mercy caused Jesus to pause for Bartimaeus' cause. The way Bartimaeus approached His Savior led to His Success in receiving His Sight. Trust me, knowing who he is and what we really need is enough to cause Christ to pause for **OUR CAUSE**.

CHAPTER 13

"Expecting the Unexpected"

"He is not here: for he has risen, as he said"
(KJV, Matthew 28:6).

THE PLANNED DEMISE and apparently inevitable outcome of the efforts of those to permanently do away with Jesus completely failed. "He is not here" is the one statement that is our "stone of hope" hewn out of the "mountain of despair."

All that had occurred and was witnessed all week long since Jesus' triumphant entry to his trumped up trial appeared to only lead to one inevitable and tragic end: Jesus' death. From the facts alone it seemed as if Jesus' fate had been forever sealed. Judging from the deeds of His executioners, and by those who rolled an immovable stone in front of His tomb, any hopes of Jesus being the Savior were now buried in the grave with Him.

The problem is that this pre-resurrection narrative only accounts for the natural occurrences. It does so because the two entities, or those parties who were responsible for Jesus' death, the Jews and Romans, were accustomed to believing that they were unbeatable forces. But they were wrong because they did not expect the unexpected nor did they understand that with GOD that ALL things are ALWAYS possible. And so it is true even after the fact, after the case has been closed, or the verdict rendered.

People always expect that their treacherous mistreatment and deceitful death blows will prevail. That's because they think that all they are dealing with is us and what we can do. They do not expect someone with greater power to intervene or to come to our rescue. The message of Easter is that no matter how it looks now, always expect the unexpected because with God ALL THINGS ARE ALWAYS POSSIBLE..... Just ask Jesus, He Got UP!

CHAPTER 14

"The Work of the Ministry"

> *"When he ascended on high he made captivity captive itself a captive; he gave gifts to his people....*
> *to equip the saints for the work of the ministry...for*
> *building up the body"* (NSRV, Ephesians 4:8, 12).

IT IS SO clear to me that the Lord intends to bless this ministry in such a mighty and demonstrative way. Toward that end, I have been praying for how to best organize our work here in Brooklyn. As a church we must not only impact individual lives but also lead those impacted lives in go forth to change others and to change where we live.

Today, as we open this ministry, we ask all to be prayerful as to how best to begin that work and to organize it so we can immediately impact others. And when I use the word WORK I mean it as used in Ephesians 4:12, as in the work of the ministry.

Now let me share with you how I want to organize our *"Five Fold Works of Ministry."* As we begin "our work of ministry" these areas of focus will serve as the basis of how we will organize our ministry.

Those **"Five Fold Works of Ministry"** are: *(1) Evangelism & Outreach*

(Lifting Jesus up and spreading the word about His life-altering soul-changing ministry; *(2) Social Concerns & Community Engagement* (as a church seeking to be the salt of the earth and the light of the world in our community; *(3) Christian Education & Spiritual Formation* (equipping the saints for the work of ministry); *(4) Stewardship* (compelling and encouraging all to give of themselves and their talents); and, *(5) Focused Ministries* (targeted ministries designed to be all things to all people according to their needs). Please pray over these and plan to inform me where you will work your work of ministry.

CHAPTER 15

"A Personal Prayer"

"I will lift up mine eyes unto the hills from which
cometh my help. My help cometh from the Lord,
which made heaven and earth"
(Psalm 121:1-2))

I WRITE AND journal my prayers. Here is one of my more recent and needful prayers. I'm transparent, are you?

"Lord, no matter how many times I've made up my mind, decided to do things differently, or decided that this would be the beginning of the last need for a new beginning, this time is absolutely different.

Why? Because as difficult as some of my past hindrances and challenges have been none of them resemble the scope and nature of this trial. Lord, I am in a fiery furnace –worse than being at the Red Sea. And in spite of the challenge I still believe that as impossible as it seems, given the sheer volume of obstacles to overcome, that my needed deliverance and turn-around can and will happen no matter how it now looks.

I've heard much encouragement from my pastoral friends, yet a part of me still wonders. I've helped so many yet how many even care. I've contributed much to what I am now enduring but I can only offer faith to overcome it. Lord, I trust you to turn it all around. I will lift my eyes to the hills and look for my help. You are MY help. In Jesus' Name. Amen."

CHAPTER 16

"When? NOW!"

*"Then you will call upon Me and go and pray to
Me, and I will listen to you. And you will seek Me
and find Me., when you search for Me with all your
heart"* (Jeremiah 29:12-13).

NO MATTER HOW long we have faced our present trials, on-going difficulties, or our wait for a change we often find ourselves wondering when will it end, when will God disclose needed directions, and even when will I have peace? And the interesting aspect of our questioning is that we act as if all of this is entirely up to God when actually it's up to *us*. It all happens when we simply say yes to Jesus when he says to us, "Follow Me."

When? Now! And for it to be NOW we have to first answer His call and answer YES to the following questions. What are your answers?

When will I totally surrender?
When will I completely yield?
When will I fully trust God?
When will I serve Him regardless?

When? Now!

CHAPTER 17

"Waiting On God"

*"But let patience have its perfect work, that you
may be perfect and complete, lacking nothing."*
(James 1:5)

PATIENCE, AS MOST of you acquaintances have probably observed over the years, was always a difficult attribute for me to possess. And quite truthfully, it was something I in some ways failed to appreciate until recently.

Most of my life I've tried to reduce the amount of time between wish and fulfillment. I've always believed that if I wanted it I should have it. And it should be now, not later. This isn't so, if I wasn't really prepared to keep it or really knew little about what was required to possess it.

Fortunately, through both divine acts and human mishaps, I've learned to acquire and appreciate patience. I've also learned the value and effect of patience and how to truly trust and wait on God and ultimately, in the process, remain physically, mentally, emotionally, and spiritually healthy. I've also learned that patience is required as God prepares us to possess His promises, prepares the circumstances to conform to His plans, and prepares people in our lives to facilitate His purposes.

Patience is simply trusting God fully and enough to be still while we wait on Him to do exactly as He has promised. It's waiting on Him regardless of the time frame, the visible opposition, and the apparent difficulties His plans might encounter in this worldly sphere and in the spiritual realm.

In my process of learning patience, and of learning to wait on God no matter how things look or how long He takes, here are a few insights I've learned about waiting on God and showing patience until He moves.(1) Things are not always how they look. Faith and patience blesses me to possess "revised vision." That is, don't try to see things as they are at any point in natural time but see what God is doing, promise-wise, regardless of how it now seems. (2) Delay is not denial. God always operates in His own time frame and not in ours. God has to take time to prepare and package His promise, to make a way for its performance, and to work on and fix us so when we receive it, it will be accepted and used for its His intended purpose and not ours.(3) God will never promise to do anything that he cannot bring to pass even if it requires human effort coupled with supernatural provision.(4) Being patient and waiting on God no matter what, who, how, or how long is the ultimate indication of the level of our faith and trust in who God really is and what He can do regardless.

Always remember that *"they that wait upon the Lord SHALL renew their strength"* and that they will not be *dissatisfied* or *denied*. So whatever the need is, wherever the need is, and no matter how difficult the need is just wait on God and TRUST in Jesus while you wait.

CHAPTER 18

Wait, Witness, and Wonder!

"Something Other Than US"

***"For the good that I would I do not; but the evil
which I would not, that I do"*** (Romans 7:19).

WHY IS IT so hard for us to admit that we are powerless, powerless
not only over those outer circumstances, but over our inward inclinations as well? I believe we have a difficult time being honest with
ourselves, even in the church, when we are struggling with apparent manifestations of sin, because we equate lack of success in this
struggle over habits, sin, and behaviors with personal weakness.

We have all heard it–when someone cannot seem to stop drinking,
stop eating, stop cheating, or simply stop sinning–the simple suggestion is offered that all they need to do is to just "make up their minds,"
"be strong," or to simply do what they haven't been able to: "just
say no and leave it alone." All of these approaches ignore the truth
that Paul points out in this passage, and that is, that there is ***something within us*** - SIN - that compels, clamors, drives, and sometimes
governs us in ways that coerce us to do things that we would not
ordinarily do–or that we do not want to do.

How many times have you continued to do something that you did not want to do, or that you constantly told yourself to stop doing, and you made up your mind daily to no longer do? Well, I am suggesting that what causes this habitual conduct, or this unending evil, is the evil one connecting with our normal sinful nature in ways that act after act develops dominion over us. And what I have discovered is that to override this innately ingrained sinfulness that seeks dominion over our lives through its fleshly feeding - it takes **SOMETHING OTHER THAN US.**

Our will alone is insufficient, our efforts unaided are unable, and a made up mind is never enough to overcome sin and to defeat its daily dominion of our lives. It takes something other than us. It takes admitting that we can't and that only God can. It takes being honest about our weakness for in our weakness we are made strong in him. Keep trying and failing on your own, or turn to God and let go and let HIM.

CHAPTER 19

"Being More Faithful"

"But this I say, He which soweth sparingly shall reap also sparingly; and he which soweth bountifully shall also reap bountifully" (2 Corinthians 9:6).

BELOVED, ONE OF the major concerns of the modern church is that its character looks nothing like the character of Christ. Christ came to give himself for us, and yet too many of us come only concerned with ourselves and our circumstance. This next holiday season, as we reflect on the selfless sacrifice of God in the form of His Son, Jesus Christ, let us ask ourselves anew, "What are we prepared to give God for all that He has given us?"

So as we shop, prepare for the holiday, and make out our extensive and expensive gift lists I thought I might add something for us to consider as believers and as New Destinites to add to our lists.

Give more of ourselves to Jesus and His Church in 2018 and beyond. We need to pause and to truthfully ask ourselves a couple of questions: "Have we been as faithful to Jesus and to His Church as he has been to us?" and, "Does what I've given to Jesus and His Church this year in any wise resemble or reflect what Christ has consistently given me?."

After we have both asked and answered these questions then let us take note and make a commitment to improving our stewardship to Him and to His Church. God has been faithful to us and it is time for us to be the same--faithful in coming, faithful in serving, faithful in witnessing to others, and faithful in giving.

So as we end this year, and we prepare to begin another, let us tell ourselves that there is absolutely nothing that can keep me away from my church and nothing and no one that can hinder me from serving the Lord with gladness here at New Destiny. I will be more faithful to the Lord and to His Church this coming year than I was in the past.

CHAPTER **20**

"Show Me The Way....."

*"Trust in the Lord with all thine heart; and lean
not unto thine own understanding. In all thy ways
acknowledge him, and he shall direct thy paths"*
(Proverbs 3:5-6).

OF ALL OF the benefits and blessings that come from God, the one
that is more important to me than most is the ability to gain guidance,
receive instruction, and be shown the way I should go by the Lord.
Consequently, as it relates to every aspect of my life my most fervent
and frequent prayer is Lord, show me the way.

This familiar text in Proverbs promises that God "shall direct thy
paths." However, upon closer inspection we discover that this promise is predicated upon our prior practice of three important spiritual
disciplines. If we need, want, pray for, and expect to receive God's
indispensable guidance then we must:

(1) **Trust in the Lord with all thine heart**. We must believe that Father
knows best and that everything we need to know, need to have, and
need to be God has. And we must trust that we shall receive the

38

provision of these needs directly from God only as we exercise and maintain our faith in Him.

(2) **Lean not unto thine own understanding**. As God reveals His plan, purpose, and path to us we must not weigh His words by our reality, look at what is as if it were the only reality, and know that no matter how wise and knowledgeable we are, God does not always reveal how he intends to do what he said he would do.

(3) **In all thy ways acknowledge him.** And as we wait to discern and discover God's will, instruction, and guidance let us persistently worship, love, and always put Him first in everything that we do, say, think, and believe. Let us, while waiting for our Word, reflect the Word we have already received and live now as one who has passed from death to life.

And if we do this: trust, lean not upon ourselves, and always acknowledge Him, God will clearly and plainly show us the way and direct our paths in ways that lead to righteousness and peace.

CHAPTER 21

Thanks Mom!

"Honour thy father and thy MOTHER, that thy days
may be long upon the land which the Lord thy God
giveth thee" (Exodus 20:12).

EVEN WITH THE unquestionable impact and influence that my father had, and still has upon me, I am a Mother's Man. That is to say, I am the man I am because of what my mother instilled in me with respect to how be a real and responsible man.

Sunday November 13, 2011, had my mother lived she would be 85 years old. I lost my mother 40 years ago in 1971 yet her influence over me is as potent, apparent, and as powerful today as it was when she graced this earth. So on each Men's Day, I honor my mother for, like many men here today who have come to celebrate our Men's Day, I would not be who I am and what I am had it not been for my mother, Mary Kathryn Sheffield. God bless you, Mom, and thanks for blessing me to be the man I am.

MARY KATHRYN SHEFFIELD

Mary Kathryn Sheffield, mother of our pastor the Rev. Horace L.

Sheffield, III, was born in Milwaukee, Wisconsin on November 13, 1926 to the late Edwin Otto and Katherine Babcock. She was a 1948 graduate of Marquette University, Marquette, Wisconsin with a Bachelor of Science degree in Nursing. Her nursing career began at the Saint Joseph Hospital, Milwaukee. Wisconsin after which she served as a public school nurse.

On January 7, 1950, Mary K. Otto married Horace L. Sheffield, Jr. in Chicago, Illinois. During her lifetime of professional nursing she faithfully and efficiently served the following hospitals: Queen of Angels, Los Angeles, California; United Automobile Workers Diagnostic Clinic, Providence, Metropolitan, and Detroit General, all located in Detroit, Michigan. At the time of her death she was the clinic director of nursing services in the PRESCAD program at Detroit General Hospital.

She was an elected member of the Detroit Board of Education; a member of the American Nursing Association; TULC: a life member of the NAACP; Michigan Nurses Economic Security Organization; Action Committee on Education. And as a great bridge enthusiast, she held membership in the Friday Nighters Bridge Club and Les Respondettes.

Mary Katherine Sheffield spent countless hours working in civic, cultural, and educational projects. One of her special interests was the diabetic children in the PRESCAD Program. She collected and distributed clothing for the needy youngsters, arranged picnics and Christmas parties--many times using her personal funds to promote her projects.

After her death a special fund was set up to keep her life's work ongoing through the Mary K. Sheffield Diabetic Pediatric Fund which continued to provide support and gifts for impoverished children who suffered from juvenile diabetes.

A GOOD WORD FOR A BETTER LIFE

She is survived by her three children: Kathryn Rose Sheffield, LaVonne Marie Sheffield, and our pastor, Rev. Horace L. Sheffield, III.

"Her children arise up, and call her blessed...Many daughters have done virtuously, but thou excellest them all. Give her the fruit of her hands: and let her own works praise her in the gates..." (Proverbs 31:28a, 29, 31).

CHAPTER 22

"After God's Heart"

"And I will give you pastors according to mine heart, which shall feed you with knowledge and understanding" (Jeremiah 3:15).

AFTER MORE THAN thirty-five years of ministry there is one fundamental and indisputable fact that I have learned about this pastoral enterprise and that is: no matter what and no matter who, God is Always in Charge.

While God's authority within the church is sometimes obscured by the behavior of believers and the self-centered nature of some, God's ultimate authority, and intentional governing of the affairs of His Church, begins and ends with His calling and placing "pastors according to (his) heart."

What that means is that God calls and then places men and women to pastoral placements not based on popularity, preaching, or personality, but based on His Heart. God calls men and women to pastor a church based on what God loves and knows is best for his people.

Too often what we do in the church, even when it comes to the man or woman of God is solely predicated on FEELING and not based on our FAITH—faith that our heavenly Father knows best. Faith that trusts that God knows more, and is better suited to see what we cannot and therefore is best able to provide what we need and not what we want.

CHAPTER 23

"A Preparational Phase!"

"In the fullness of time, God sent His Son...."
(Philippians 2:14-15)

OFTEN THAT WHICH we seek is not being denied; it is just being delayed. All the good, all of what we have longed for, prayed for, worked toward, and sought after is not being withheld; it is simply being postponed so that we may complete and fulfill an imposed preparational phase.

This preparational phase can be seen in just about everything that God does. Before God created Adam and Eve on the sixth day, he prepared paradise for them. Before Israel could inherit her promise and take possession of the land flowing with milk and honey, that is their promised land, they had to endure forty years of wandering within the wilderness. And before you, I, or anyone else was born we completed a preparational phase in our mother's wombs.

So with everything there is a preparational phase that occupies the space of time between wish and fulfillment, work and outcome, and prayer and answer. Consequently, it sometimes becomes so easy to view this lapse of time between wish and fulfillment as God's indifference or as the shared vision being thwarted and circumvented.

Just maybe it is neither. It might just be God waiting for either the appointed time, or waiting to ensure that what he bestows upon us, and gives us we have been properly and completely prepared to receive.

God's people wanted, prayed for, and looked for a Savior. However, before God sent his son, the chosen people had to wait, had to experience life without an intimate relationship with God, and had to learn to long for what once was--God being a present help in their time of trouble.

In this interim period, when the people of God had to wait, they were being prepared to receive God in the flesh first through patriarchs, then prophets, and finally priests. While all these provided some means of relating to God none alone could provide a relationship with God.

God made his people wait, pray, and long for being able to be one with Him alone through Emmanuel. All of those who preceded the preeminent during this preparational phase only one prepared the way for Jesus the Christ.

Beloved, New Destiny, our wait is over; God has come in the flesh in the form of his Son Jesus the Christ. As we prepare to celebrate his birth let us prepare ourselves, our ministries, and our church to receive as if we have long been awaiting his arrival.

Let us celebrate Him as God's gift to us, and let us give others the same sense of newness that we have received through him. The wait is over, He has come.

CHAPTER 24

"A Model Church"

"Then they that gladly received his word were baptized; and the same day were added three thousand souls. And they continued steadfastly in the apostles' doctrine and fellowship, and in breaking of bread, and in prayers....Praising God, and having favour with all the people. And the Lord added to the church daily such as should be saved" (Acts 2:41, 42, and 47).

THOSE OF US who are in the leadership of the church, and others of us whose heart is here with this church, often find ourselves wrestling with how to make New Galilee better, how to get people who on one Sunday seem so sincere when they join, to come back and to sustain their enthusiasm for the church and for the Lord. At times we wonder whether if what we do as a church and as a gathered group of confessed believers has any impact on any of the above. In essence, is there a model for our church that New Galilee can embrace, adopt, and follow that will address all of these circumstances that contend with our congregation?

The answer is that there is a model church; it was the New Testament church which began on the day of Pentecost. What were the standards, the behaviors, the disciplines of this early church that resulted in the Lord adding *"to the church daily such as should be saved"* (Acts 2:47). Before I list and discuss them, let me argue now that this same set of standards and incorporation of disciplines of the early church are the very same ones that are required today for us to likewise achieve and sustain numerical and spiritual congregational growth. Now, what were those successful standards, behaviors, and disciplines of the early church that made them so successful? From the text above let me suggest three.

(1) *They gladly received "his word."* No church can ever prosper if it is not hungry for the Word of God. Sure, we love music, the fellowship, and all that our churches offer, but if there is no Word--no hunger for the Word--then it is a gathering without God and a church without Christ.

(2) *They continued steadfastly.* Too many of us come to the church seeking emergency relief from an impending crisis, and, once whatever was threatening subsides, we disappear. We are to be urgent in season and out of season. We cannot treat God like a secondary consideration when he demands to be our primary focus.

(3) *They governed the nature of their interpersonal interaction.* When they came together they didn't bicker, gossip, grip, and spend time complaining. No, they fellowshipped (broke bread), sought God's presence in their lives (prayer), they worshipped (praised God), they governed how they treated one another (had favour with all the people), and as a result of their Christian conduct and character they became the "Soul Saving Station" as God added to the church daily such as should be saved.

Why don't we try this same approach at Our Church?

CHAPTER 25

"Membership or MINISTRY".....
By Pastor Sheffield

> *"THEREFORE SEEING we have this ministry, as we have received mercy, we faint not; But have renounced the hidden things of dishonesty, not walking in craftiness, nor handling the word of God deceitfully; but by manifestation of the truth commending ourselves to every man's conscience in the sight of God. But if our Gospel be hid, it is hid to them that are lost"* (II Corinthians 4:1-3).

ONE OF THE things that I wrestle most with is to what degree do we as members of a church see what we do, what we say, and how we behave when we interact with each other as *ministry*, and not merely membership? To me this is an important distinction, the difference between membership and ministry. It is important for this reason: if we see our conduct and service, and what we do here in church, as simply membership and not ministry, then what we do and how we do it is governed by a different set of standards than ministry.

Membership is transient--we are here today and gone tomorrow.

Ministry is not intermittent. We are engaged in it for a lifetime: everywhere, in everything, every word, every act, and in every commitment we make to serve in the choir, as a deacon, as pastor, or as the custodian. Paul makes this point indisputable when he exclaims that since "we have this *ministry*", not since we are members or have this position, *"we faint not."* Ministry is not based on everyone seeing what God has shown you, it's doesn't wait till others possess your sense of mission and urgency before you serve, and ministry knows for whom the service to His Church is rendered; it is given to God and for those to whom the Gospel is hid.

And furthermore, I am also always baffled by how *"blessed folk,"* (at least that's what they testify to be) who have "received mercy" can be so easily sidetracked and kept from ministry. Those of us who had no legs of our own left upon which to stand, and yet God stood us up, God has called us to ministry and not just membership. He did not bring us out and call us in just to sit here and witness the work of the Holy Spirit. No, God wants us to do *His ministry.*

And what is that *ministry*, it is to live and to witness in this church and in the midst of this fellowship, in a way that gives godly evidence that we *have* "renounced the hidden things of dishonesty" *(not doing things in the dark and behind someone's back)*, that we are "not walking in craftiness" *(not involved in organized antagonism and membership mayhem)*, and that we no longer "handle the Word of God deceitfully" *(quoting it but not studying or living it)*. **Believers, when we do MINISTRY- that's when the Gospel is no longer hid to those who are lost.**

CHAPTER **26**

"A Time To Be Thankful"

"But thanks be to God, which giveth us the victory
through our Lord Jesus Christ."
(I Corinthians 15:57)

THERE IS SO much, if we allowed ourselves to be distracted by this world, that would adjust our attitude of gratitude. Often we let our physical condition, the deeds of others, conflict with our neighbors, a struggling and depressed economy, our social environments, what's going on in our homes, in our churches, and even our challenges with our children trump the truth that we are to, no matter what, be thankful to God who has already given us the victory through Jesus Christ.

Saints, **BE THANKFUL** - for no matter what it is that we are contending with, where that struggle takes place, who it is that is desperately and deliberately trying their best to antagonize our opportunities and block our blessings, and regardless of whether or not, right now at this moment, you're winning or losing any of these battles in your personal war to prevail against the enemy, just know that the outcome has already been predetermined. **YOU WILL WIN - YOU ALREADY HAVE THE VICTORY.**

These truths, while evident all year long, are especially on my mind during the Thanksgiving season. While America is grateful for the Pilgrim's arrival, who discovered a land that was already someone else's and then made it theirs, and for the bounty and prowess of this nation, wealth which has often been gained at the expense and exploitation of others--I am grateful for something so much more important that status, possessions, and power placement in this world.

I am thankful and grateful to God, that I have the victory through Jesus. I am thankful to Jesus Christ for giving me the victory over the wretched man that I am. I am thankful to Jesus Christ for giving me the victory over the dominion of sin and over all of the forms by which it has manifested itself in my flesh throughout my life. I am thankful to Jesus Christ for giving me the victory over the wiles of the devil. I am thankful to Jesus Christ for giving me the victory over the assaults of others who say and do things which, if unaided by Christ, I would perhaps angrily and violently respond to. I am thankful to Jesus Christ for the victory over _____. You fill in the blanks.

CHAPTER 27

"HUSH!"

*"Do all things without MURMURINGS
and DISPUTINGS: That ye may be
blameless and harmless...."*
(Philippians 2:14-15)

SO MUCH OF what happens whenever people gather in one place is affected, influenced, and governed by what comes out of their mouths. The mean, judgmental, often untruthful clandestine undercurrent of conversation within a congregation--that is, what people in church have to say about one another, eventually surfaces and often does harm to the person talked about and can even wreck and destroy a church.

This verbally running people down is not a new phenomenon as it relates to the destructive impact it has on any unit of people who are joined together for whatever reason. Families throughout history have been separated because of something cruel that was said. Nations have gone to war and killed millions of people over a few mis-spoken and accusatory words; And churches have spoiled the spirit, negated the work of Christ, eagerly driven people away from the fellowship, and all but kept God out of their churches because of their ungodly gossip and unmindful murmuring.

Terrible clandestine comments, and secretive negative expressions about others, deliberately designed to be said behind the back of the person being discussed, antagonize, crush, undermine, uproot, and destroy people's lives. Let's be clear, biblically, murmuring, talking against Moses, God, and one another, is what kept Israel in the wilderness for forty years. For this cause most of those who left Egypt never arrived in Canaan. God seemed to be ready to change his mind about the Hebrew children altogether had it not been for Moses' mediation. And Moses was the one they ran down the most, yet he pleaded with God to spare them and to give them another chance.

Paul understood the power of anonymous acrimony--Ill feelings and conversations about others that were carried on about someone behind their back. There are several other places where the Bible tells us how to deal honestly with others (get a concordance and do some work looking these up yourself):**(1)** if someone is overtaken in a fault ye who are spiritual restore such a one, considering yourself; **(2)** do not receive false witness; **(3)** be slow to speak; **(4)** if you have aught with that person go to them, if they do not receive you go back with a witness; **(5)** by judging others you will not escape judgment yourself; and **(6)** bear each other's burdens.

We have much biblical direction with respect to how we are to deal with one another if we have an issue or a problem with someone in the church. Yet we still choose to hold gossip sessions with others about people, and we still have our mouths instead of our hearts all over our brothers and sisters in the Lord. Beloved, if we were really concerned about the spiritual and emotional well-being of those who we freely discuss with others in and outside the church, we would minimally go to that person and share our concern, and then perhaps, if you really want to demonstrate Christ-likeness, love them and pray for them.

Paul says to the church at Philippi, keep your mouths off of each other and work silently. Worship and work without murmuring. Hush, hold that word. Hush, do not be a part of private and personal discussions about your pastor, your choir member, or anyone in the church. Hush, hold that word. Hush, do not tell someone else the hearsay someone just sinfully shared with you. Hush, do not smile in your brother or sister's face and then talk about them behind their back.

Paul is saying, "Beloved, if you, as a member of New Galilee, as a saint in the church of the Jesus Christ, can hush and cease to murmur and to dispute then, and only then, you will be *blameless* and *harmless*. If you want to contribute to the church, do so by adopting and adhering to a standard of care for one another that as a must incorporates a commitment not to harm anyone with what we say.

And know that those who continue to run people down instead of lifting Jesus up--much will be said of them. Not by us but by Jesus as he argues for their judgment based on the number of little ones that they have caused to stumble, and as he remains true to his Word of judgment "those who show no mercy shall receive no mercy." HUSH!

HUSH!

CHAPTER 28

"A Pentecostal Experience"

"Then they that gladly received his word were baptized; and the same day there were added unto them about three thousand souls" (Matthew 16:18).

IN AN ERA in which churches are frantic about finding proven approaches to achieve and sustain church growth, many of which are worldly models glossed over with Gospel embellishments, if we at New Galilee seek the same, we need to simply look to the WORD of God for both our means and our method. The greatest church growth *ever* took place on one day, the day of Pentecost, at the conclusion of Peter's preaching, when God added about 3,000 souls at one invitation, at one opening of the doors of the church. And brothers and sisters, I believe that whatever God has done, he can STILL DO, even at New Galilee!!!

Let us take a brief and summarized look at those things which occurred prior to the nearly 3,000 joining that led to, facilitated, laid the ground work, and made it possible for this to happen and for these "new members" to continue steadfastly in the Apostles' doctrine. Here is what occurred on Pentecost that made it possible for this phenomenal church growth.

(1) **The Disciples were Obedient.** The disciples, despite their disappointment with Jesus and displeasure with one another, went to Jerusalem as Jesus had instructed them. Once there, in one place, and in one accord (in spite of whatever their issues might have been) God empowered them FIRST with the anointing of the Holy Ghost. Had God not done this, then faltering and denying Peter could not have stood up and openly preached about the same Jesus he had not so long ago denied. Beloved, when we obey God we can do things we could not otherwise do!

(2) **Once the Leadership was Empowered they Exalted the Name of Jesus Christ.** With all of the people gathered, this changed crowd of disciples, who were just a few moments earlier a gang of ordinary Jews in an upper room, were now able to stand up in the marketplace in the midst of the people who had been responsible for the crucifixion of Christ and they witnessed to His Lordship. More importantly, regardless of any threat to them personally, they openly identified themselves with Jesus. And of course, it was Peter who forsook Jesus and fled, who being most bold in his proclamation said, "Therefore let all of the house of Israel know assuredly, that God hath made that same Jesus, whom ye have crucified both Lord and Christ." To grow we must exalt Jesus.

(3) **The Holy Spirit Created and Sustained Unity.** It is no small miracle that all of these different people: Parthians, Elamites, Phrygian, Arabians, and Cretes, once the Holy Spirit came upon them, could hear each speak their own language. Here were all these people in one place, from different classes, some rich and some poor, and from different cultures, some Jews and some Arabians, and yet they could all hear each other, could all hear the same thing, and eventually all would see Jesus as the same: their Savior.

(4) **Listening to the Word led to Living for the Lord.** Again, here were these people, the same people who had recently participated

57

in killing Jesus, having just attempted to rid their land of his presence and power, now hearing an empowered, transformed Peter preaching Jesus. Their hearts were so pricked by the WORD they began saying in response to Jesus, "Men and brethren, what shall we do?" And, of course, Peter was prepared for he told them, "Repent, and be baptized every one of you in the name of Jesus Christ for the remission of sins...." Now, let us not lose sight of how the Word transformed this crowd, for Peter and the disciples who were once sought after by these same hate-filled people who treated the disciples like criminals--the Word now tells us--are saved and are referred to as "brethren." That is to say that this crowd, once full of hatred, having now accepted Jesus as Christ, were full of love.

(5) How They Started is How They Stayed, and How They Ended. These believers, who we are told "gladly received his word" and who were baptized did not start and then stop serving the Lord. No, the Bible says that they continued steadfastly in the Apostles' doctrine, fellowshipping, praying, and breaking bread together. For a church to grow we must fellowship with one another and become one.

(6) Now the Church Can Grow. With all of this firmly forming the foundation of the church, empowerment of the Holy Spirit, unity of the believers, establishing who Jesus is, and continuing to teach and fellowship, God could add daily "to the church such as would be saved." New Galilee, once we are at this place God will do all of that.

CHAPTER 29

"I'm Growing Weary"

*"And let us not be weary in well doing: for in due
season we shall reap if we faint not"* (Galatians 6:9).

LIKE SO MANY other sayings, adages, insights, and scriptures, this
suggestion of Paul's not to become weary is based on the visible realities of our personal and collective condition, far easier said than
done.

As pastor, I personally think of all that God has blessed New Galilee
to be and to do: build a new church, have hundreds of people confess Christ and join every year, develop the Safe Center and Children
of Tomorrow After School Program, rescue and care for our members.
Then I look out at our pews and often see only a marginal membership in attendance. **I get WEARY in WELL DOING.** As a person who
is not immune to circumstances and is not untouched mentally, spiritually, and emotionally by the ups and downs of our fellowship, when
I look at how much we, as a church, have sacrificed to give to others
and yet we still struggle in all ways. We still only see a seemingly
small core group of committed and dependable saints who do most
of the church's work, I wonder, "How Long, O Lord Before We Truly
Prosper As A Church?"

I am tired and becoming wearied in well doing. And the only thing that can change that is if YOU, Y - O - U help this church to prosper and to grow in the following critical ways: **(1)** by modeling personal behaviors and treatment of others that reflect Christ-likeness; **(2)** by evangelizing and recruiting others for Jesus and for this church; **(3)** by becoming more familiar and concerned with who is here and who isn't, and seeking to maintain each other in fellowship with one another; **(4)** by personally helping to build, to grow, and to prosper the various church ministries through your personal participation and active support; **(5)** by being sincere about the seriousness of your personal contribution and stewardship of time, talent, and money to the church; **(6)** by coming to church on a consistent basis not just every now and then; and **(7)** by becoming personally dedicated and individually involved in regularly helping the church membership to grow.

Help us grow this church. We've been to-o-o good to to-o-o many people for our church not to be full and flourishing every Sunday. **Help me not to be wearied in well doing!**

In The End

(A Poem by Rev. Horace Sheffield)

The true measure of a life well-spent
Will not be measured By where we sit
But by how well we serve!

It will not be weighed
By how popular we are,
But how principled we live.
It will not be judged
By where we have been,
Rather by where we end up!

At the end....All of our
Money will be non-negotiable,
Our status non-transferable,
And our power non-respected!

At the end...the true measure
Of a life well spent
Will not be determined
By how much we have,
But by how much we give!

At the end...will
Your End Be An End Or
A New Beginning?

CHAPTER **30**

"Marked by Baptism!"

*"Go ye therefore, and teach all nations, baptizing
them in the name of the Father, and of the Son, and
of the Holy Ghost"* (Matthew 28:19a).

BAPTISM HAS BEEN a practice that has been used by many faiths as an initiation or allowance of access into a particular faith. In the Christian Church, we baptize only those who are old enough to publicly confess with their mouths the Lord Jesus Christ as their Savior. Therefore, as Baptists, drawing on the life of Jesus Christ, who was baptized by John the Baptist in the Jordan as an adult, we do not engage in pedobaptism--that is, the baptizing of babies. In this regard, again, we follow the example of Jesus Christ, who did not send children away; instead he blessed them. Hence, in the Baptist church we dedicate, receive, consecrate and bless children.

What is baptism? Well, simply put, it is the sacramental rite which admits a candidate into the Christian Church. Furthermore, according to the Apostle Paul, baptism represents: **(1)** the believers' mystical and literal union with Christ through which he or she participates in Jesus' death and resurrection (Romans 6:4); **(2)** for the person submitting, it serves as a cleansing from sin (I Corinthians 6:11); and, **(3)** the act by which we are incorporated into the Body of Christ (I Corinthians 12:13).

Today, as in the past, certain people believe that based on which church, which ministry, or which minister performed the rite that a person's baptism may be null and void. Well, to refute this claim, Augustine, a great and early theologian of the Christian Church, established the validity and affect of baptism regardless of the worthiness of the minister or the church. In the Latin this teaching is known as **non cogitandum quis det, sedquid det**. So in other words, the affect of baptism has everything to do with the candidate's surrender and submission to Jesus Christ and nothing to do with the person performing it or the ministry sanctioning it.

There have been many teachings about baptism based on mode--Immersion or sprinkling, or based on pronouncement—is it in Jesus' name or in the name of the Father, the Son, and the Holy Ghost? But the one which I cherish most is the **Doctrine of Baptismal Character** developed by **Hermas,** and taught by **St. Cyril of Jerusalem**, both of the early church. The Doctrine of Baptismal Character teaches us that baptism *"marks the soul"* through a sanctifying grace so as to place a seal upon it which remains and makes it "recognizable by both God and the devil."

What Hermas and St. Cyril believed and taught I have come to know as true through my own personal experience and those of many of the people for whom I have been a pastor for years. Baptism marks us and sends a signal to the one who has suppressed and oppressed us that we have been freed from the dominion of sin and that we now belong to God. This marking is why the devil's darts are magnified and intensify once we accept Christ and are baptized. Once we're baptized, the devil SEES us differently because we have been marked by the Master. But take heart, this seal and mark now also allows God and Jesus to see us differently—for now we belong to God and what belongs to God he protects, he fights for, he keeps up with, and he gives the victory to.

CHAPTER 31

"A Visible Display"

"When Jesus saw their faith, he said unto the sick of the palsy, Son, thy sins be forgiven thee" (Mark 2:5).

THERE IS AN observable difference between simply saying you want to be delivered and being at a point and prepared to doing anything to achieve it. So many times, the only time that we even discuss deliverance is when the consequences of our choices catch up with us - and then the only way for us to soften our sins - at least in the eyes of others - so we think, is to say "I need help."

In this passage, clearly this sick person, who was physically challenged, needed both spiritual and physical help. However, unlike so many, he was prepared to go out of his way to do whatever it would take to free himself, and to be freed. This is why we find him here in this text seeking any way he can to encounter Christ - that Jesus may heal him and deliver him.

First, this sick man was not dissuaded by the large crowd, and others who were there before him, who were waiting too on Jesus and had filled every inch of the room Jesus was in. Instead of this sick man returning home and saying - "the rehab center would not take my insurance", or "that the line was too long to access my breakthrough - he'd never get to me," this weak, sick, and physically-challenged man, in need of deliverance, refused to leave the same way he came.

This sick man - and those with him banded together - because he had enough of being bound. Enough was enough. He was sick and tired of being sick and tired. He was determined to be freed that day from his bondage of physical and spiritual oppression. Therefore, he set out to - no matter what - see his Savior so that Jesus could assist him in shattering his strongholds. So this man - unable to get through the doorway, unable to get into the room where Jesus was ministering - decided that he had to be delivered, that day, so with some help he climbed the walls of the house that Jesus was in - tore the roof off - and was lowered down into the sight of the Savior. His visible display revealed his determination to be delivered - not tomorrow- the next week - but that day

God is waiting for our visible display of how determined we are to gain our freedom from the dominion of sin in our lives. He's waiting for us to fight our demons to have our cords cut, waiting for us to tear roofs off, to hound him, to insist on his touch, and to stop at nothing to be seen, to be set free, and to be completely healed by the Savior. Are you ready to be free? I am!

CHAPTER 32

"Ignorance is Inexcusable"

"Study to show thyself approved unto God, a work-man that needeth not be ashamed, rightly dividing the word of truth" (II Timothy 2:15).

EVEN A CURSORY examination of the natural history of man will reveal that we were once slaves to irrational behavior, and subject to unfriendly notions of the cosmos. Over time, rational man came to understand his world, and this universe, better and what man once feared, deified, and was severely subjected to, he now came to understand, and in some instances used for the benefit of mankind.

This quest for understanding and pursuit of a better understanding of man's environment was furthered by curiosity, study, discovery, and learning. It was curiosity, study, and discovery that led Pythagoras to conclude that the earth was round and not flat; it was discovery and study that led Galileo to prove that the earth rotates around the sun not the sun around the earth; it was discovery and study that led Einstein to postulate the Theory of Relativity; and it was discovery and study that resulted in Dr. Charles Richard Drew becoming the first person to set up a blood bank, and to discover that blood plasma could take the place of whole blood transfusions.

Likewise, the only way we can truly intimately know God beyond just a Sunday morning worship service acquaintance is through discovery and study. First, we need to learn of the Lord from where He has been primarily disclosed or revealed to us - and that is - In His WORD. And then, for us to Learn of Him and to Know Him - we must adhere to this scriptural admonishment to "Study to show thyself approved...."

Learning about God empowers us to be free from superstition and the enslavement to other's suggestions about who God is and how God works. Learning about God produces freedom from fear for "God hath not given us a spirit of fear..." Learning about God equips the saints of God and the Body of Christ (Soma Christos) for Christ-centered ministry and interpersonal relationships. Learning about God will convince you that you cannot both please man and please God. It's time for New Galilee, and those of us who worship here, to take time to educate ourselves about the Ways of God, the Calling of Christ, the Move of the Holy Spirit, the need for true fellowship among the saints, and how each of these transforms us into Christ-likeness - for ignorance is inexcusable and intolerable as well!

CHAPTER 33

"No Place Lide Home"

"Let's have a feast and celebrate. For this my son was dead and is alive again; he was lost and is found" (Luke 15:23).

I HOPE AND pray that all who I now know, have ever known, and will ever know will at least learn one lesson that I know is true, and that is, that there is no place like home!

Most of us were just like this impatient prodigal son. We too, just as soon as we became adolescents, immediately thought we knew more than our parents. Oh yes, we thought that we could handle anything we decided to do, even if others before us and around us, who thought likewise, had damaged and destroyed their lives doing the same. Armed with our youthful arrogance some of us proudly made our painful pilgrimages into our far countries of self-indulgence, self-centeredness, disobedience, social estrangement, and flight from God.

And many of us, at least those that are not still stuck somewhere in the mud, again like this father's son in Luke, one day awakened, came to our senses, and realized that our decisions had led us to a dark, dead end alley, and that our dreams had become nightmares. Simply put, at least for me, I came to the realization that what I already had and already was - was not something to destroy just to prove others wrong, prove that I could be independent, and prove that no one could stop me from doing whatever I wanted to do - even if it led to my ruin. In my course of surveying the far country, leaving behind my upbringing, what was instilled in me - I discover, as did the prodigal, on the eve of my personal end that there was and is no place like HOME.

And where is home? Home does not simply encompass where you were raised, but how you were raised. Home isn't limited to where you lived, east side or west side. No, home is how you were raised to live. And for me, given the times in which I was raised, home was a place where God was, where you experienced a loving Jesus, and where you were taught to commit yourself to something more than just you. Home was where you were taught to abide by a set of time tested moral principles like honesty, respect, cleanliness, godliness, and such behavior that our parents firmly believed shaped one's character. Home was where our parents, siblings, God, and I lived. There was - and there still is no place like Home. Home is being back with God. Home is with God!

CHAPTER 34

"God By NAME & NATURE!"

"...for I am the Lord that healeth thee..."
(Exodus 15:26).

HAVING TO RECENTLY wrestle with the news that someone that I love very dearly was diagnosed with cancer, and not instantly knowing the precise and particular prognosis for her recovery from the medical profession, I was tempted to despair. For a moment, for a collection of hours, for perhaps even a day or so I suddenly was not the preacher reaching for words to use to comfort others, I was a person searching to make sense of this situation for myself. For a few huddled hours, I was not the pastor fellowshipping with a mother of my congregation who had a son - trying to foster her faith, I was a brother bothered and beleaguered by seemingly the threat of another potential loss among my already shrunken family. I was now not only dealing with despair - but sinking in sorrow - and saying to myself "woe is me, I am utterly undone."

But as God has done in comparable circumstances, when it seemed my end was nearer than my beginning, He spoke to me concerning my family's present plight - and simply said, Horace, Son, Skippy, *"I AM THE LORD THAT HEALETH THEE."* Now know that I was not immediately relieved for I was not seeking my healing but the healing of my sibling. As I thought this, God read my mind and said - "Who I am I will be to them - and What I have done for others I will do for them."

God had to remind me that we are the ones who are territorial and self-focused. God was speaking to me and reminding me of both His Name (Yahweh) and His Nature (Healing). These truths about God which will they are immutable - unchangeable - are thankfully transferable. Proof: in this Exodus passage Yahweh (meaning a God who focuses on personal relationship) is speaking to Moses and the Hebrew people. Since that time God has spoken these same words of healing to others, and I believe He is speaking them now to my loved one, as he spoke them to me, to Violet Ramsey, and to others you and I both know.

God says, I am the Lord (this is my name) who healeth thee (this is my nature)! So then Lord, be who you are and do what you do - **HEAL US, LORD?** Heal us Now! Heal our brokenness, our sinfulness, our pain, our wanderings, our relationships, our spirits, and our BODIES!

This is my prayer, today, tomorrow, and forever more.

CHAPTER 35

"Storms Happen"

I RECENTLY READ, in a book entitled *"The Life God Blesses"* by Gordon MacDonald, about a South African Christian who had lost all in his quest to oppose apartheid. Evidently, he and his family had been targeted for retribution and retaliation by white racists. As a result of his fervent stand, he and his family had been violently taken from their home in the middle of the night and were forced to watch as it was gutted and burned to ashes.

Nothing was left following this attack. All of his belongings, furniture, clothing, books, and sermons were gone and nothing but ashes and a horrid memory of the attack and the abuse were left.

As his friends gathered to give him comfort they noticed that on the chimney wall which still stood, he had taken the very ash of the remains and had written these words, addressing God, in defiance of his attackers:

"Put me to what you will.
Put me to doing,
Put me to Suffering,
Let me be laid aside of you,
Let me have all things,

Let me have nothing.
I freely and heartily yield
All things to your pleasure and disposal."

When your storm rises - will you so yield - **ALL THINGS AGAIN** to God's pleasure and to His disposal?

CHAPTER 36

Rules of Engagement and Terms of Service
(Authored by Pastor Sheffield)

Please be informed that in accordance with a divine directive received from my direct supervisor - GOD, *Effective Immediately*, the following stipulations apply to all members. NO APPEALS WILL BE HEARD!

(1) If you WON'T or DON'T do the WORK, You CAN'T have the JOB!

(2) No SWEAT Equity, No SPEECH Equity!

Signed: GOD

CHAPTER **37**

"Raising Children"

*"And straightway the damsel arose, and walked; for
she was of the age of twelve years"* (Mark 5:41).

THIS TWELVE-YEAR-OLD CHILD that Jesus took by the hand and
raised from the dead was Jairus' daughter. She had died while her father, Jairus, attempted to do everything, including trying to find Jesus,
to save her as she lay at the point of death. Yet all of Jairus' best efforts
failed—and before Jesus could come to her bedside she died.

The Bible tells us though, that this is really the beginning of the story
and not the end. For when Jesus arrived at Jairus' house, greeted by
grief, weeping and wailing, he did what we need to do with our own,
he took her by the hand, spoke to her situation and raised that child
from the dead.

Today, I write these words from the pastor, because just as Jesus did
- I believe we also are responsible for *"raising children"*. When I was
in Tennessee, on the Children's Defense Fund's Alex Haley Farm, I
heard Dr. Tenney, from Virginia Union, describe what happened
to him when one of his high school students was shot and killed.
Dr. Tenney said that while preaching this young man's funeral, and

admonishing the congregation to care for this mother in the loss of "her child," that the Holy Spirit spoke to him and expressed that the reason these deaths continued to occur unchecked is that we see the victims as someone else's child and not our own. Dr. Tenney said that with that revelation he stopped his sermon and said to the church that this young man is not just her child he is "my child," and that from that day forward, Jesus did so with Jairus' daughter. He was going to take it upon himself to be engaged in *"raising his children," from whatever*, whether he birthed them or not, so that he would not have to bury children.

I thought about the funeral of the young man that I preached here on Wednesday, who died from gunshot wounds. The culture of violence snuffed his life out - and also held hostage many of those here in attendance at his funeral. I asked myself, *"How can we as a church be involved in raising our children?"* To raise our children we must see them as **OURS**, not the deacon's and not the trustee's - **BUT AS OURS**. I do not want to pray for the power to raise any of our children from the dead, but I do want the power to be responsible for them as if they were my own. New Galilee, we need to be about **RAISING OUR CHILDREN**! Not waiting to raise them from the dead, but raising our children NOW into a newness of life--into a life of peace and infinite value. Please decide to Raise Our Children - before we have to bury another one!

CHAPTER **38**

"Something Other Than US"

"For the good that I would I do not; but the evil
which I would not, that I do."
(Romans 7:19)

WHY IS IT so hard for us to admit that we are powerless, powerless not only over those outer circumstances, but over our inward inclinations as well? I believe we have a difficult time being honest with ourselves, even in the church, when we are struggling with apparent manifestations of sin, because we equate lack of success in this struggle over habits, sin, and behaviors with personal weakness.

We have all heard it—when someone cannot seem to stop drinking, stop eating, stop cheating, or simply stop sinning--the simple suggestion that all they need to do is to just "make up their minds," "be strong," or to simply do what they haven't been able to: "Just say no - and leave it alone." All of these approaches ignore the truth that Paul points out in this passage, and that is, there is **something within us** - **SIN** - that compels, clamors, drives, and sometimes governs us in ways that coerce us to do things that we would not ordinarily do or that we do not want to do.

How many times have you continued to do something that you did not want to do, or that you constantly told yourself to stop doing, and you made up your mind daily to no longer do? Well, I am suggesting that what causes this habitual conduct, or this unending evil, is the evil one connecting with our normal sinful nature in ways that act and after act develops dominion over us. And what I have discovered is that to override this innately ingrained sinfulness that seeks dominion of our lives through its fleshly feeding it takes **SOMETHING OTHER THAN US.**

Our will alone is insufficient, our efforts unaided are unable, and a made up mind is never enough to overcome sin and to defeat its daily dominion of our lives. It takes something other than us. It takes admitting that we can't and that only God can. It takes being honest about our weakness, for in our weakness we are made strong in him. Keep trying and failing on your own or turn to God and let go and let HIM.

CHAPTER 39

"The 3 S's of CHURCH SUCCESS - Acts 2:41-43"

"Then they that gladly received his word were baptized: and the same day there were added unto them about three thousands souls..." (Acts 2:41).

PASTORS, MINISTRIES, AND church leaders around the world pray and search for a way to make their churches grow and succeed. Often, in this quest to be bigger and better, those who search for formulas to grow their churches simply observe others and attempt to do what they have done. While every church and its ministry is different I believe that there are three (3) core cornerstones that must be embraced and practiced for a church to be successful. Those three core cornerstones are seeking, surrendering, and serving.

(1) *SEEKING* (Acts 2:41). "Then they that gladly received (GK., *dechomai*, to receive by deliberate and ready reception what is offered) were baptized." For our church to succeed we need to be full of believers who faithfully search and seek for God and then without reluctance receive and follow him. And our search for him should be as relentless and persistent as a thirsty man needing water to survive in a dry desert.

(2) *SURRENDER* (Acts 2:42). "And they continued (GK. *dia pantos*, the period and time frame throughout which something is done) steadfastly in the Apostle's doctrine and fellowship...For too many seekers our search ends once the trouble and trials cease, or until we gain the minimum from the master. Discipleship, or following Jesus, is not a short term preoccupation, it is a lifelong all-consuming occupation. If we are to succeed in ministry we must continue steadfast in our coming, our giving, and in our serving.

(3) *SERVING* (Acts 2:43). "And fear came upon every soul: and many wonders and signs (GK., *semeion*, that which distinguishes one person from others) were done by the Apostles." We seek and we surrender but for one reason: to seek God and to serve His church. So many come in here in emergency status, in dire despair, and in great financial and social need and our seeking and serving last only until we are rescued or find relief. God is looking for people who feel a debt of gratitude and a commitment to serve God that will last a lifetime and will persist though plagued and problematic.

There are 3 S's of success, and embracing these will achieve sustained church growth.

CHAPTER **40**

"Trust or Technique"

"Lord, give us strength to trust you when life's burdens seem too much to bear; dispel the darkness with new hope, and help us rise above despair"
(C. Spurgeon).

THERE IS NO question that no matter how well we live, how faithful we are to an ethical and moral lifestyle, and no matter what psychological approach to life we embrace–there will come a time for all of us when life seems too much to bear. This fact is true for us and it was even true for Jesus who, in the Garden of Gethsemane, realizing the extent of the sacrifice he was about to make for others, asked if he could be relieved of his responsibility to redeem the world.

So, then, we can all agree that all arrive at a place in our pilgrimage where and when "life's burdens seem too much to bear." Spurgeon, who wrote these words, suggests, in the words above, two discernible ways to deal with this burdensome place: (1) "give US" – tells us that we are not to face our burdens alone. For us not to drown in despair and become independently affected individuals we are to approach them as we do prevailing prayer–as two or three gathered together–praying with and for one another; and, (2) displace the darkness with new hope. The only way one sentiment, perspective, circumstance, or feeling will leave us is for us to replace it with another.

Finally, Spurgeon makes it crystal clear that our ultimate aim, if we are down, is to "rise above despair." Psychologists tell you that to do this you need technique (therapy, medication, or positive peer approaches). Preachers, I tell you, to achieve this, you need TRUST. Psychologists, through counseling, help you deal with circumstances. Preachers, through your prayers and trust in God, **help you change circumstances.**

Barbara Brown Taylor, in her book *God In Pain*, suggests that to rise above despair, and to get out of what we have gotten ourselves "stuck" in we must not "substitute our own expertise for the power of God." Simply put, freedom, the shedding of new light and the changing of circumstances only comes about through TRUST IN GOD, not the reliance upon our own techniques. Trust God, not techniques!

CHAPTER 41

"For Goodness' Sake"

TRACING PEOPLE'S MOTIVATION or, that is, trying to figure out why people do what they do has become a big and popular business. In fact, the fascination with discovering what led to a certain act, what caused a certain conduct, and why someone behaved in a certain manner often gets more attention than the act or behavior itself.

And so in essence the curious question, as it relates to some bad act, almost always is, "Why did she do that, or how did that happen?" And so if our community can ask why did someone act ill, then we as a church should also ask, "Why do we do good?" I used to ask this question of my parents, who insisted on certain high ethical and moral behaviors or conduct that was almost always different from the action of others. And the answer I always received from them was, "Son, you do good - just for goodness sake."

We, as born again believers, and as stewards of God's manifold grace should do good for the sake of the good itself. In other words, we do good for the investment not the return or for the act not the outcome. We do good for the very nature of the activity, which happens to also be the nature of the God we serve: merciful, kind, long suffering, just, and loving.

Too many of us, when it comes to doing good, whether it be in the church, with our family, or to others become emotionally short-circuited, blow our psychological fuses, and sometimes simply and flatly refuse to persist in doing good because of the improper response, reception, and resistance to us and our gifts.

In these instances, let us do good as Jesus did good, regardless of the wrong done to us, because our reward comes from God and is not found in the response to us from others. "Beloved, let us do good to all and especially to those who are of the household of faith" (Galatians 6:10).

CHAPTER 42

"Blessed Now & Blessed Later"

"These things are written, that ye might believe that Jesus is the Christ, the Son of God; and that believing ye might have life through his name."
(John 20:31)

EVERY EVENT, EVERY circumstance, and every spoken and written word seeks to serve some purpose; often both an immediate one and one which endures. This is also true for the setting forth, writing down, and the binding together of miracle, historical facts, and theological teachings within the Gospel of John.

Unlike some materials that we read, and we wrestle with to discover and discern their meaning, John eliminates our need to search for the reason for his writing. John makes it quite clear that "these things are written that ye might believe." John wrote his Gospel that we might believe " (Greek, believe/pistis, be persuaded, be won over), that we might be won for Christ and be persuaded that Jesus is the Son of God.

Specifically, John asserts that the whole purpose of his book is to win us over, that we might believe that Jesus is the Christ, and the Son of

God. John wants us to embrace his discovered truth that all the promises of God have been, are being, and forever will be fulfilled though Jesus Christ, who is the Son of God. John wants us to believe that the Jesus he knew and witnessed, who was born in a manger, who died on a cross, and who rose again from his tomb is God himself in the flesh. Therefore, the search for full revelation is now over because everything we need to learn and know about God, about being obedient to the cross, and how to live totally for God can be answered by Jesus.

Furthermore, John suggests that this discovery divulges a certain outcome. John says that once we believe that our belief leads to "life (Greek, zoe) through his name" and that this means that through our belief we are personally indwelt by God. This acquired life through His name is not only a blessed life in this world, but believing in Jesus leads to a *mellousa* (Greek) blessed afterlife even in the one which is to come. That is Jesus, and our belief in Him: a blessed life now, a blessed life later, and a blessed life for evermore.

CHAPTER 43

"If I Am Wrong Please Tell Me"

"A fool despises his father's instruction, but he who receives correction is prudent." (Proverbs 15:5)

IT HAS BEEN said of me that people are afraid to approach me and to talk to me! Perhaps it's because of the way people approach me. It is difficult to receive criticism from someone who does not do the very same thing that they are telling you to. Or, sometimes it's hard to handle correction from someone who only criticizes and who never compliments you for anything. Well, let me set the record straight: I am finally in a place where I do not bristle at, nor am I antagonistic toward anyone who wants to criticize me, so long as what is said is intended to help me, assist me, develop me, improve me, and to make me better and for others who can benefit from me and are blessed by me.

Lately, I have realized how much I have grown in this regard, in terms of receiving correction and a critique, when someone very close and special to me, who has been here since I came to New Galilee, told me how much they enjoyed last Sunday's sermon, "I Won't Complain." In our discussion about the sermon, I asked her if enjoying this sermon more than most meant that she did not enjoy the others? Her answer simply was "No, I just didn't understand the others; this one, I could really relate to and understand!"

Now, not so long ago I might have taken her statement as meaning that she just didn't like my preaching, or wondered why it took her twelve years to tell me that she didn't "like" my preaching. Instead, learning to be wiser, I probed her response further, wanting to know what was it about this sermon that connected and enabled her to understand what I was saying? I wanted to know this so I could learn and understand where I might be going wrong. Thus, I could make it right and preach more often in a way that was more easily understood.

Criticism isn't always a put down; sometimes it is intended for our improvement. This is especially so when it comes from someone we know cares. So today, church, if I am wrong don't tell others, —tell me so I can help you to understand what I'm doing, why, and hopefully do it better.

CHAPTER 44

"I Believe"

I *BELIEVE* THAT just because two people argue, it doesn't mean they don't love each other. And just because they don't argue, it doesn't mean they do. I *believe* that we don't have to change friends if we understand that friends change. I *believe* that no matter how good a friend is, they're going to hurt you every once in a while and you must forgive them for that. I *believe* that true friendship continues to grow, even over the longest distance. Same goes for true love. I *believe* that you can do something in an instant that will give you heartache for life. I *believe* that it's taking me a long time to become the person I want to be.

I *believe* that you should always leave loved ones with loving words. It may be the last time you see them. I *believe* that you can keep going long after you think you can't. I *believe* that we are responsible for what we do, no matter how we feel. I *believe* that either you control your attitude or it controls you. I *believe* that heroes are the people who do what has to be done when it needs to be done, regardless of the consequences. I *believe* that money is a lousy way of keeping score. I *believe* that my best friend and I can do anything or nothing and have the best time. I *believe* that sometimes the people you expect to kick you when you're down will be the ones to help you get back up.

I *believe* that sometimes when I'm angry, I have the right to be angry, but that doesn't give me the right to be cruel. I *believe* that maturity has more to do with what types of experiences you've had and what you've learned from them and less to do with how many birthdays you've celebrated. I *believe* that it isn't always enough to be forgiven by others. Sometimes you have to learn to forgive yourself. I *believe* that no matter how bad your heart is broken, the world doesn't stop for your grief. I *believe* that our background and circumstances may have influenced who we are, but we are responsible for who we become. I *believe* that you shouldn't be so eager to find out a secret. It could change your life forever.

I *believe* two people can look at the exact same thing and see something totally different. I *believe* that your life can be changed in a matter of hours by people who don't even know you. I *believe* that even when you think you have no more to give, when a friend cries out to you, you will find the strength to help. I *believe* that credentials on the wall do not make you a decent human being.

I *believe* that the people you care about most in life are taken from you too soon. I *believe* that you should send this to all of the people that you believe in. I just did. The happiest people don't necessarily have the best of everything; they just make the best of everything they have.

CHAPTER 45

The Idea and the Reality

"Bear each others burdens and so fulfill ye the law"
(Galatians 6:2).

WE HAVE A great challenge before us as a congregation. As a church, members of the body of Christ, we have been called to care for, to be compassionate toward, and to express and display love for those who among us, who at any time along their personal paths, may find themselves with their backs against the wall.

Perhaps it involves being bashed by betrayal, trapped by trials, sullied by sorrows, ensnarled by economic woe, challenged by disrespectful and disobedient children, poisoned by a negative perspective, or maybe wearied by an unrelenting struggle and fight with cancer – nonetheless, whatever it is that our members are burdened by we are called to respond and to assist them in bearing it.

Beloved, let's be clear: our responsibility, based on John 9, is not to chance circumstances (that is, to try to discover the cause of the condition). No, our Christian duty is to, even if only by our mere presence alone, try to heal and to change the conditions in which we find others. And we can only change conditions by being attentive to the needs of others, being aware of the plight of our people, to know the burdens others bear and to help carry them as a church.

Whatever it is, however it is, whoever it is – we have been given a sacred assignment, and a God-given task to do as the Lord instructed his prophets to do, that is, to "comfort ye, comfort ye, my people," and to also do as the Apostle Paul admonishes us to do – simply and consistently to "bear each other's burdens."

Bear each other's burdens, that's it, and that's all. Bear, *aino* in the Greek, means to take up, to place upon oneself, or to take it away; and, burden, *boros*, again in Greek means to relieve the pressure of a heavy load. As New Galileans, and as obedient followers of Christ, by bearing each other's burdens we likewise take upon ourselves the burdens of others and we relieve the social, emotional, economic, and spiritual pressures of our brother and sister in the Lord.

As I close, there are four among us who so need this burden-bearing assistance. They are Sis. Violet Ramsey, Bro. Charles Mercer, Sis. Latosha Patterson, and Bro. Patrick Fitch. Let us, as lovers of the Lord and lovers of one another, persistently strive to bridge the gap between Paul's admonishment to bear and care and our actual practice, and the gap between the idea of bearing and the reality of caring. So let us be and do, Amen.

CHAPTER 46

"A Real Father"

For this my son was dead, and is alive again...."
(Luke 15:24a)

REAL FATHERS IN the present African American family life and experience are an endangered species, if not almost extinct. Unfortunately, it appears that more and more Black men, at an alarming rate, are content to merely serve as sperm donors than parental providers, and are more aptly characterized as "baby boys" than real men.

Real fathers have a deep-rooted inner sense that they must be there for their children, and that no one has to make them do for their seed. Real fathers will bear any burden, face any foe, and sacrifice even of life to ensure the protection, the provision, and prosperity of their children.

Sociological suggestions, anthropological arguments, cultural crisis, and prejudiced perspectives notwithstanding, Black males today are less responsible for themselves, and for others related to them, than were our forefathers who were more oppressed and less educated than we are.

So as to not merely be descriptive but prescriptive, let me suggest that the only way to overcome these harsh realities is for us as fathers to live up to our God-given responsibilities toward our children. And toward this end I thought I would outline and provide us with some spiritual principles to guide our fathering. According to the Bible fathers are:

To Love (Genesis 37:14)

To Command (Genesis 50:16)

To Instruct (Proverbs 1:8)

To Guide and Warn
(I Thessalonians 2:11)

To Train (Hosea 11:3)

To Rebuke (Genesis 34:30)

To Restrain (I Samuel 3:13)

To Punish
(Deuteronomy 21:18-21

To Chasten (Hebrews 12:7)

To Nourish (Isaiah 1:2)

To Meet Their Needs (Matt. 7:8-11)

To Not Provoke
(Ephesians 6:4)

How many men here today who have shared sperm are truly REAL FATHERS?

CHAPTER 47

"Magic or Mindset"

"So we built the wall: and the wall was joined to-gether unto the half thereof: for the people had a mind to work" (Nehemiah 4:6).

CHURCH PEOPLE TEND to look at how to prosper, how to achieve success, and how to fulfil a vision for a congregation in one of only a few ways. First, there are those among us who are waiting entirely on God's initiative and effort, without any help from them--except maybe to watch and wait to bring the vision to pass. Secondly, there are others in our midst who believe that their sheer will, personal preparation, and acquired skill sets alone, without any divine assistance, can get the job done. And thirdly, there are others here with us who seemingly care less if the church prospers or not as long as they can personally exact (get from) from the church the narrow selfish gain they came to achieve. And the third, unlike the two above, are neither waiting on God, nor doing any work themselves.

Listen, beloved, for a church, for New Galilee to prosper in ministry it takes an acquired mindset not magic. Magic is waiting for people to come who we have never even invited. Magic is expecting the church to meets its financial obligations when we don't tithe, give on a regular basis, or give at all. Magic is waiting on the choir stand to be filled with us still sitting in the pews. Magic is wanting a new car and you don't ever go to work to earn a dime to purchase it. And, magic is wanting something but doing absolutely nothing to get it. In this text, the people of God, facing the destruction of their temple (church), decided that to achieve its rebuilding they had to work and not wait on magic. They knew that they had to have a mindset to work and not a reliance on magic.

Magic would have been to sit down under the shade of the tree and watch God build it; mindset told them to look at what needed to be done and for each of them to commit themselves to personally doing it. They had a mind to work and not to rely on God alone but to daily doing their part (and praying that God would bless their efforts). They had a mind to work; and in each instance of personal conflict to look beyond themselves and to focus on their goal. They had a mind to work; to achieve their goal of glorifying God through the house they were building and to build it themselves and not to look to someone else to do it.

New Galilee we need a mind to work--to build up His House and His Ministry, to prosper in this place that he made provision for us to build, and to lay aside any weight which may impede its construction.

New Galilee - so let us also have the right mind and Build Up His House, New Galilee.

CHAPTER **48**

"Do So For You"

"My times are in thy hand: deliver me from the hand of mine enemies, and from them that perse-cute me. Make thy face to shine upon thy servant: save me for thy mercies' sake" **(Psalm 31:15-16).**

GIVEN THE BROAD scope and range of life's experiences, the ups and downs, the pitfalls and pains, the antagonisms and annoyances, and even the appearance of misfortune and opposition, sometimes it's hard to still believe that our times are in God's hand. Perhaps our problem is that we have confined God to only be responsible for the good and for him to be absent in the bad!

Well, it is apparent that David did not hold this perspective. In fact, to the contrary, David begins these two verses by reaffirming his belief in God's ultimate and unparalleled power and authority over him and his affairs. David says to God, "my times are in thy hand." If David didn't believe this then there would be nothing that God could do about any of the agonies he was experiencing. Likewise, New Galilee, if you do not believe that our times are in God's hands - then there is little that we can expect God to do about any of the things for which we so desperately need God's help.

I believe that my life, your life, and the life of this congregation and their time, that is, all that affects and involves each, are in God's hands and God's Alone. That's why I, like David, believe that there is absolutely nothing that invades my space, occurs within my personal sphere, or that I am exposed to that God does not have supreme authority and dominion over, and is causing to work together for our good.

"Lord, New Galilee, Pastor Sheffield, the Last Chance Academy, and all of your people here are in your hands. Deliver us from our known and secret enemies, jealousy, assault and attacks on our character, from them that persecute and violate us, and from anyone and everything that would impede our perfection. And Lord, make your face to shine on us, your servants, that we may be aided in our kingdom-building endeavors and our personal pursuits.

Finally, Lord, save us not because we deserve it, not because we are so good, or better than others, and not because we are entitled to such, but do so for you, for your mercies sake. Do so that others can see it and know that you are who you say you are: merciful, forgiving, and still in charge.

CHAPTER **49**

"Home Schooling"

"Train up a child in the way he should go: And when
he is old, he will not depart from it."
(Proverbs 22:6)

EVERYTHING THAT I know, everything that I am, and everything that I believe I learned in my mother and father's and grandmother and grandfather's house. In fact, I never will forget how important this learning, that is "home schooling," was to my grandfather, Horace Lindsey Sheffield, Sr. My grandfather was superintendent of Sunday School for the Tabernacle Baptist Missionary Church in Detroit for over forty years, and in his position was often asked to speak there and in other churches. He would keep his audiences spellbound with his wisdom and biblical insight. But every time he spoke, as he closed and before he sat down he would always say:

> *"Children, I didn't go to Harvard and I didn't go to Morehouse. What I learned I learned in God's house and my mother's house, and I have a Ph.D. in human psychology and I learned in the classroom of life. And I am just trying to plant my footprints in the sands of time."*

What my grandfather attested to, and was also my experience, is just a product of plain home-schooling. If there is anything missing today in terms of our children's behavior, and the behavior of grown folks, it is that they were not taught what my generation was taught at home. Nor do they embrace the notion embedded in this text--that if you as a parent instill something in your child, or children, when they are young (train up a child) they will not depart from it.

We cannot expect our children to behave better when they are out, are in school, or are in church than they do when they are at home. Instruction, direction, correction, and discipline must start early and must be so impressed upon a child that it becomes a part of their DNA. It is hard for someone to do something, or to be something, or to behave in ways that are contrary to the character that has been cultivated in them since they were children. Do not try to change them once they are grown or have adopted and acquired destructive ways. No, train them up now, set a correct course for them now, and then you do as you would have them do.

CHAPTER 50

"It's Up To Us"

By Rev. Horace L. Sheffield, III, Chairman,
National Black Leadership Commission on AIDs –
Detroit Chapter
(Written for the Michigan Chronicle, Special Insert)

OF ALL THE current and past challenges that African Americans have been forced to face over the last two hundred years, including lynching, Jim Crow, the KKK, the deliberate destruction of our nuclear and extended families, and racial profiling, most if not all of these have been caused and compounded by societal and racial forces. However, today, the most life-threatening community crisis that we face as African Americans is something that we are responsible for and that our choices contribute to, and that is the uninhibited spread of HIV AIDS. And unfortunately if we as a people persist in failing to rise up and respond to this community health crisis there'll be no need to address systematic poverty, racism, or economic exploitation by the larger dominant society because very few of us will be healthy enough or even alive to enjoy such social, political and economic gains. What we do about this pandemic and what happens to us is not in the hands of the CDC (Center for Disease Control) it's in the hands of you and me!

Right now, in cities such as Detroit, New York, Flint and Syracuse it is our people, our sons and daughters, our church sisters and brothers, black people, who despite the national and local prevention and treatment focus who are both the most HIV AIDS affected and infected population, and the most at risk for becoming so. Why are these facts the case? Because in our community HIV AIDS ignorance still prevails! Our churches, our pastors, our leaders, and many of our people still see this disease as one that primarily affects the white gay male population and not ours, and they are quick to point to their particular homosexual behavior (and now to the black gay male) as the primary cause for the disease's spread. Well, all of this is absolutely not true. Presently, African Americans, and most notably African American women, represent 52% of all reported HIV AIDS cases and are the most at-risk population in America. And it is not others' behavior that is the cause for this spread among our community – it is ours!

How can African Americans be the most at risk HIV AIDS population in America? It is so because of our unsafe and unethical sexual practices! Despite a preponderance of messages about African Americans being at the greatest risk for contracting HIV AIDS, our people still apparently prefer pleasure over protection. I travel often to Nassau, Bahamas to visit Bishop Delton Fernander and the New Destiny Baptist Church and I am amazed about how seriously the Bahamians take this HIV AIDS and sexually transmitted disease crisis. All over the radio, on their highly visible billboards, and even in their churches they have launched a safe sex campaign telling Bahamians to ***"Protect Ya Tings, Man!"***

Yet right here in our own community – one more affected by HIV and AIDS than Nassau – we seem content to sit back and witness our innocent children, our women, and our families become decimated daily by this disease, and then we still regularly do not practice safe sex –which is the one almost certain way to stop its deadly spread.

And, most tragically, our women are unknowingly being exposed to this dreaded disease by the unethical practices of their lovers who are simultaneously engaging in same and opposite known and confirmed disease-laden sexual relations and behaviors.

And most unfortunate of all are the hypocritical voices in the church who have condemned the affected and who often ask those with HIV AIDS, "Who did sin?" Well, what about that faithful married woman who has never slept with anyone but her husband and whose only sin may have been letting him back into her bed, exposing herself to HIV AIDS, without knowing that he was both low down and on the down low. How hypocritical for preachers to condemn our people for their sexual practices when sometimes ours remain in question, and how horrendous for preachers to judge others for being affected with HIV AIDS when many of us engage in risky same and heterosexual sexual behaviors and have died (even though the official cause was said to be otherwise) from the same. Who and what will we continue to blame as more of us publicly succumb to a similar fate?

For me the argument and the debate cannot be focused on why folks died. It must now be focused on how we can and must help others to live, and not on who is to blame. The discussion must be directed toward a broad and all-encompassing community response and a changed public policy that ensures our permanent exclusion from the "most at-risk" category. An all encompassing compassionate community response and a forced change in HIV AIDS public policy are the two twin tenets of BLACA's approach toward addressing and abating the spread of HIV AIDS within the African American community, and in Detroit. We need to mobilize our communities and our churches to respond. After all, no one else really cares whether we live or die. We must alert others to this risk, for no one else will endeavor to sound an alarm in our community about how great a risk this actually is. They didn't do so when it affected white gay men either. No, white gay men organized, changed their own behaviors and then challenged and changed public policy and subsequently secured funding to both prevent and treat this disease among their affected and most at-risk populations. And today, they have gone from the most affected to the least at risk. We need to borrow their approach – act-up, act-out, and then collectively permanently move ourselves out of this category of being the most at risk and the most affected.

And for this to be, the Black Church must play its part and embrace responding to the HIV and AIDS pandemic, and the saving of our lives, as fervently as it pursues redemption and salvation. *It is up to us* to save ourselves and to stop the awful spread of this dreaded disease. *It is up to us* to stop taking such threatening personal risks with our health that ultimately imperils and kills others. It is up to us to stop the spread of HIV and AIDS in our community. Therefore, right now, I challenge churches, sororities, associations, and block clubs to come and join with BLACA and to help us to say to HIV and AIDS, and to those at risk, that **"DEATH CAN WAIT."**

CHAPTER 51

"Rising Above Despair"

"I will lift up mine eyes unto the hills, from whence
cometh my help, my help cometh from the Lord"
(Psalms 121:1).

EARLIER THIS WEEK, as I do every morning, I was in my prayer closet seeking God again for counsel and reading through various devotional materials when I came across these words written by Charles Spurgeon:

"Lord, give us grace to trust you when Life's burdens
seem too much to bear; Dispel the darkness with
new hope, And help us to rise above despair!"

What a powerful and apt spiritual approach, through prayer, to help us rise above despair. All of us, no matter what our appearance or what we say, have moments when what we are dealing with seems more than we can bear. --Wwe face instances when life appears more against us than working for us; or even worse, times when the nature of the worldly circumstances we are forced to contend with are such that even our Christ-centered connection fails to alleviate our agony.

In instances, situations, circumstances, and dispositions comparable to those in the Psalms, both Spurgeon and King David, make it quite clear that for us to rise above our immediate despair we must look away from what ails and look to He who only can assist us. And we look to God, and to Jesus, like Spurgeon who in his prayer specifically requested that God dispel the darkness and help him rise above despair. We too, when we go to our God and find Him in our secret place, must be specific about what we need to do to rise above our personal despair.

We too, like Spurgeon, must pen our prayer to address our despair and our darkness. "Lord, dispel the darkness of my despair with new hope that, no matter how dark it gets, morning will come; Lord dispel the darkness of my lost love with the new hope of a love from you that never ceases and cannot be interrupted. Lord dispel the darkness of my earthly betrayals with the new hope of fellowshipping with a friend in Jesus that remains as close as a brother; and Lord dispel the darkness of a factitious fellowship with the new hope of a new joy rooted in our interactions with one another. Lord, help me to rise above despair."

CHAPTER **52**

"Here To Help You"

"Therefore I endure all things for the elect's sake,
that they may also obtain the salvation which is in
Christ Jesus..." (II Timothy 2:10).

EVERY CIRCUMSTANCE, TO determine its real value, must be taken
in its complete and overall context. Likewise, some experiences, left
to stand alone, may on their face seem adverse, detrimental, and even
potentially destructive and harmful. However, if we were to connect
our circumstances, join our experiences, and weigh everything that
happens to us in the light of some grander good, and eternal purpose
then what may have initially seemed hurtful may actually end up being helpful.

Paul, in this familiar passage, provides us with a particular perspective that, as saints who seek to serve a divine purpose within a social
context (the church), we should seek to enhance and to employ. Paul
says, "I endure all things for the elect's sake," which means that in
church we should not think solely of ourselves—rather think of how
what we are forced to face in the fellowship serves some greater purpose for those who witness our perseverance. Consequently, I am
prepared to endure pain if it results in someone else prospering, ready

to endure ridicule if it results in someone else's redemption, set to deal with hardship if it helps others see and gain heaven, and willingly to submit to suffering if it ultimately means that someone else will be saved. Our problem today in the church is that too many are here only for comfort, gain, and personal progress and will not sacrifice anything to see someone else gain.

All of us should be like Paul, prepared to endure all things if it means someone else will be blessed from my buffeting. I am not here for me. I do not come week after week blind to the plight of others, and so self-absorbed that what affects others has no affect on me. I come to church every week prepared to suffer, ready to be rejected, set to be slain by others, primed for persecution, and expecting to endure hardship willingly if in the end someone besides me can experience what I have enjoyed and share the salvation I have been so freely given.

At New Galilee, we, like Paul, must prayerfully prepare ourselves to "endure all things" if it means others will be blessed and saved as a result. I will gladly go through any trial if it results in someone else's transformation. How about you?

CHAPTER **53**

"Saved or Sidetracked?"

WITH SO MANY challenges to the church, crime, decadence, and moral and social decline evident everywhere, those of us who have a relationship with Jesus Christ call ill afford to be sidetracked and diverted from discipleship.

So many of us have developed ridiculous justifications for being sidelined and sidetracked from our personal responsibility of both accepting Jesus Christ, responding to his claims, and faithfully serving Him and one another. Often we get sidetracked from our salvation because we have issues with the pastor, because we feel mistreated by the membership, or we feel as if the congregation has failed to allow us to exercise some God-given gift, even if it is in some self-centered way.

Of course, none of us, even the church, has obtained perfection, and neither have you. It is insane to continuously point a finger at others and to blame them for your failure to be a good steward. To do this is simply allowing oneself to become sidetracked and not necessarily saved. Blaming Pastor Sheffield, blaming Bro. George O'Neil, or blaming whoever for whatever you perceived as being the cause of your cessation from obeying God will not nullify nor negate your responsibility to give God an account for your deeds and misdeeds.

Beloved, it is always easier, and clearer to see, the faults of others than it is to see one's own. Nonetheless, never let the faults, frailties, and failures of others sidetrack us from our eternal purpose, and to sideline us from our ministry. Sidetracked saints are different from saved saints.

Sidetracked saints see everything that is wrong; saved saints assist Jesus in the process of making everything right. Sidetracked saints are folks focused only themselves and only on how their gifts are not being used; saved saints see how God is in the midst of it all and only concern themselves with how God is using the committed to do everything. Sidetracked folks are bound and governed and affected by what others do, don't do, say , and shouldn't have said; saved folks are only governed and only focus on what Jesus has done, is doing, and has promised to do. The question is: are you sidetracked or are you saved?

CHAPTER **54**

"No Less Than God"

"...for He makes His sun rise on the evil and on the
good, and sends rain on the just and on the unjust"
(Matthew 5:45b).

ISN'T IT AMAZING how we profess to be Christ-like, which is in essence to be like God--- and yet we act so ungodly. How is it that we expect God to extend this matchless mercy toward us in our mistakes yet we withdraw the same toward others in their shortcomings?

How do we dare decide who should experience the grace of God and be allowed in His presence? If the truth be told, based on our behavior, we should be banned from even mentioning his name. What am I trying to say? I am suggesting that in our conduct, in our character, and in our conversation, if we profess to love God and to be acquiring Christ-likeness, we should treat others no less than God does!

How does God treat others? Well, this text tells us that he is indiscriminate. He doesn't only provide for the good but he makes allowances for the evil as well. He does not just make certain that the just are sustained, he ensures that the same rain nourishes the unjust. Now, if God goes out of his way to treat all he has created with mercy, why are we so quick to treat miserably those who live differently, believe differently, and who have made different choices than us.

Beloved, when it comes to others, regardless if they rich or poor, black or white, straight or gay, we always should treat people no less than how God has admonished us to. We should treat them no differently than God has treated and is treating us. And we should respond to them just as God, who knows all about us, responds to us.

Even more, we are called to likewise love them as God loves them. We should try to reach this point and place in our pilgrimage in which the only thing that we see when we look at others is God's cherished children. If God makes certain that he is inclusive of everyone in His care regardless of our proclivities, predicaments, and problems, we should do no less than God and be mindful of others without respect to their faults, failings, or frailties.

Whatever we say, whatever we do, and however we treat each other, it should be no less than how God has and is with us.

CHAPTER 55

"Lord, I am Yours!"

"Lord, take my life and make it wholly Thine; Fill my poor heart with Thy great love divine. Take all my will, my passion, self, and pride; I now surrender, Lord, in me abide" (Orr).

WHAT A POWERFUL prayer of supplication and submission. And what a perfect time of the year, when we eagerly sacrifice to give others material gifts, for us to seriously consider giving ourselves completely to Christ. On the last Sunday of the year, I thought that this powerful prayer would be a good basis by which to discuss our gift of ourselves to Jesus Christ. The giving of such a personal gift of self sentiments and soul simply begins with the simple affirmation, now made directly to God, **"Lord, I am Yours!"**

"Lord, take my life and make it wholly Thine." Lord, as I surrender, I give you permission to override my inclinations, to subdue my passions, and to transform my tendencies - simply <u>take</u> and then <u>make</u> my life "wholly Thine." Otherwise, unless you <u>take</u> and <u>make</u> me fully, I may well continue to be halfhearted, unevenly yoked, and to persistently and perpetually place others and other things above and ahead of you. **"Lord, I am Yours!"**

"Fill my poor heart with Thy great love divine." Lord, all of my hell, habits, hardships, and hatred have found a home in my heart and consequently tend to manifest themselves in my conduct and my character. In my innermost parts, and in the hidden chamber of my poor heart, I need you to dislodge my decadence, devilment, and despair and replace them with your transcendent presence, or in other words, I need you, instead of me, to live and dwell fully in my heart. Then, when this occurs, I will love right, walk right, serve right, talk right, do church right, and even live right because you, Jesus, will live in me and govern my heart.

"Take all my will, my passion, self, and pride; I now surrender, Lord in me abide." Jesus, please conform the components of my character to resemble a Christ-like composition and no longer an ungodly creation. Each and every part of me--which now works independently to achieve my divine disobedience--I ask that you would cause to cooperate with your plan to achieve Christ-likeness in me and with me. "Lord, I am Yours!"

"Lord, I am Yours!" I need to be; I pray to be; I want to be; I come to church to be; and I absolutely have to be! Lord, make me completely yours - today - this morning - right here and right now! Amen.

CHAPTER **56**

"Wanted: Faith For Tasks"

*"Behold, I will do a new thing; now it shall spring
forth; shall ye not know it?"* **(Isaiah 43:19)**

THE UNPRECEDENTED ELECTION of Sen. Barack Obama as the 44th
President of the United States of America is further proof that God is
doing a new thing. Not only has the paradigm changed for our political life, that is the way things are done, but there is also a clear prophetic and spiritual change that God is bringing to pass in the Body
of Christ (soma Christos). It seems to me that God is saying, as he just
indicated to this nation, "Behold, I will do a new thing."

What is this new thing that God is doing in the church? God is changing the focus of the church from merely worshipping Him to faithfully
and completely serving Him. God is changing our emphasis from us
asking and receiving from him, to us giving ourselves to Him, to others, and to His church. God has been so good to us, which we readily
admit, but what has all that goodness done for the church, for our
communities, and even for the countless brothers and sisters of ours
who struggle alone to deal with their difficulties without any tangible
help from us?

"Behold, I will do a new thing..."God says. The new thing that I am doing is looking for believers who have faith to perform tasks, change other's lives, and not just faith enough to ask for more things for themselves. God wants to transform the landscape of his believer's lives and to reclaim this earth as sacred space. And to do this it will take a refocused faith from us that looks beyond ourselves and concentrates on us, personally alleviating the agony and aggravation of others. God is tired of us asking for things- things that once we get them we don't even use for Him, for others, or to transform the church. God is getting wearied with is worrying him to help us when we don't help anyone else ourselves. God is growing impatient with us pleading for him to ease our pain and all we do is cause others and the church the same.

God wants us to have faith for tasks; the task of changing the culture of his church; the task of molding the lives of young people into selfless servants of this church and community; and, the task of building up His church as a place of transformation, committed Christian workers, and benevolent care.

CHAPTER **57**

"What Are Your Options?"

"And we know that all things work together for good to them that love God, to them that are the called according to his purpose" (Romans 8:28).

IT IS ALWAYS easier when trouble becomes our twin, problems our parents, sorrow our son, and despair our daughter to think that the universe and the environment are aligned against us. It is understandable to wonder, when the only associate you have is adversary and your constant companion is confusion, if everything in the created order has been issued an assignment against you.

Fortunately, Paul decided centuries ago to help us clear up any confusion about how we should perceive our problems and encounter our negative experiences. Paul declares that "all things are working together for good - to them that love God, to them that are called according to his purpose." Paul expressly and intentionally did not say that adversary would not visit, or that pain would not persist, that evil would end, or that difficulties would not say hello to us early every morning. No. What Paul did say, through this text, is that twists and turns, no matter how terrible and turbulent, are transformed by God so that their natural affect are divinely diminished and they now ultimately assume a better and good purpose.

So, today, I want you to know you have, I have, and all of us, based on this text, have two options related to how we choose to view vicissitudes, perceive problems, and to size up our sorrow: (1) To see death, circumstances, economic crisis, betrayal, and painful events as being at odds with our purposes; or, (2) To see all of this and whatever else is unfortunate, distasteful, and unpleasant as actually and ultimately cooperating with the will of God to achieve His intended purpose in and with us.

I do not know about you, I choose the latter option. That is to see every situation and circumstance as something God works with for my good. If I do this then like Joseph my option is to believe that while others meant evil - God means good. If I do this then, like Paul - even though persecuted and plagued by problems I can choose the option of believing that regardless God is able to keep that which I committed unto Him until the last day. And if I choose this option then, like Job, I can exercise the right option and affirmation - no matter what - and say the Lord giveth and Lord taketh away.

CHAPTER **58**

"Having A Little Talk With Jesus"

"Be careful for nothing; but in everything by prayer and supplication with thanksgiving let your requests be made known unto God!" (Philippians 4:6)

GOD KNOWS THAT in most instances, and seemingly at all times, that I am forced to deal with things that no human unaided could ever handle alone. Often, when these responsibilities are multiplied, I get stressed even though I clearly know that I am blessed. Recently, I've discovered that every time I get sick and my immune system is compromised that it is directly related to having to handle an inordinate degree of difficulties and being saddled with an overwhelming load of burdens.

Church, this is why I love the hymn *"I Must Tell Jesus"* so much. *"I must tell Jesus, I must tell Jesus; I cannot bear these burdens alone. In my distresses he kindly will help me, Jesus will help me, Jesus alone!"* I have learned that the only way that I can handle my cross so heavy to bear, deal with complicated and conflicting circumstances, and persevere through pain and persecution is to daily, incessantly, and continuously have a little talk with Jesus.

Here are a few things, which I will elaborate on later in future writings, that I regularly take to the Lord in my daily prayer.

(1) Lord, help me to regularly realize that I am not completely responsible regarding what will ultimately happen with New Galilee. **(2)** Lord, these temporal matters have taken me to the brink of inner turmoil and emotional exhaustion; revive, preserve, refresh, and restore me while in your peaceful presence. **(3)** Lord, help me not to concentrate so much on the agonies that have regularly aligned themselves against me that I fail to focus on the fact that I am more than a conqueror over all things through YOU.

Whatever you are presently going through, whoever it is that is antagonizing you, and however things presently appear to be, always remember that a little talk with Jesus makes everything all right.

CHAPTER 59

"Let Me Spare You Your Effort"

"This is a faithful saying, and worthy of all accepta-
tion, that Christ Jesus came into the world to save
sinners; of whom I am chief" (I Timothy 1:15).

LET ME SPARE you the effort of trying to uncover any mess on me, of trying to find out the scoop on my character, dig up some dirt, and of the need to further spread any guile you heard about something I supposedly said in pastor's Bible class. I have no problem admitting that I am wrong most of the time, whenever you say that I am; that even though I have confessed Christ I still struggle to be conformed to Christ-likeness; and, I am one of those **sheep** in the "all we like **sheep** have gone astray."

Like Paul, I readily and openly confess that Christ Jesus came into the world to save sinners, "of whom I am chief," or that I am one of the primary beneficiaries of this blessed grace and a regular recipient of mercy. Me, Horace L. Sheffield, III, am not where others pretend to be. I still struggle to do right, I still struggle not to sin, and I still need help from God to be more God-like and to do right most of the time.

Unlike so many "great pretenders" in the church and in our social spaces, I am what I am and what you see is what I am. I do not carry on a Sunday act just for the church. I do not look down on others and pretend to be on some holy and higher level than everyone else. I am here in church to respond to God's convictions not man's condemnation, and to openly confess, that is agree with God, as to what my faults and sins are before God.

So again, let me spare you the effort to spy on me, to overhear what I say and then embellish it, change and alter it, and then pass it on to others in such a way as to degrade me and portray me in some negative light. Let me spare you your efforts to make me less than blessed - because like you - I know that I am just a SINNER saved by GRACE. No one has to point that out nor prove that to me. I know better than you what I am and what I am not.

What about you? Maybe you were saved by your personal merit, redeemed by your impeccable righteousness, and did God a favor offering yourself to Him. Keep living - keep pretending, and keep not acknowledging your faults while highlighting the sins of others - and before you know it GRACE will NEED to become your best friend.

CHAPTER **60**

"There is Much To Be Thankful For"

"I will bless the Lord at all times " **(Psalm 34:1).**

HAVE YOU EVER taken time to think about just how much God has done for you? Have you paused, even in the midst of trials and tribulations, just to thank God for His goodness? The songwriter Jonathan Oatman, Jr. in his famous hymn *"Count Your Blessings,"* spoke to this when he penned these words: "When upon life's billows you are tempest tossed, When you are discouraged, thinking all is lost, Count your many blessings-name them one by one, And it will surprise you what the Lord has done."

I wonder, have you ever made a list of what the Lord has done and what you are thankful for? This past week, while in retreat in my personal prayer closet, I thought about a few things that I am thankful to God for through Jesus Christ. You should make a list, here's mine.

I'm THANKFUL to GOD FOR:

(1) Being governed by and under grace.

(2) Being managed by mercy.

(3) For the 3 P's (Protection, Providence, and Promise).

(4) For all the innumerable instances of God's intervention

(5) For the undeniable details of my deliverance

(6) For my children, though they are sometimes challenging

(7) For my family who are both living and deceased

(8) For the daily proofs of His provision

(9) For always being a very present help in time of trouble

CHAPTER 61

What Are You Thankful For? Tell Him, Not Just Me!

"A Word on Michael Jackson"

TUESDAY JULY 7, 2009, I attended the Detroit Tigers v. Kansas City Royals baseball game at Comerica Park on what I later learned was Elvis Presley day. How strange, and even contemptuous, it was I thought for the Tigers, and its mostly white audience to honor Elvis Presley as their King on the same day that Michael Jackson, the real King of Pop, was eulogized..

At first, after talking to several African American Comerica Park employees, I was angry as I was led to believe that the "Elvis Presley Day" was an impromptu celebration designed to counter the celebration and adoration that our community, and the world, was so vividly displaying over the death of Michael Jackson. Actually, I was mad and I was going to call my friends the Rev. Al Sharpton and Rev. Jesse Jackson and we were going to picket and protest until the Detroit Tigers became the Detroit Kittens. However, later I learned, after speaking with someone from the Tigers organization, that the Elvis Presley day was set and on the Detroit Tigers published season calendar since March 2009.

Nonetheless, the significance of Elvis' day taking place on the same day of Michael's funeral wasn't lost on me. Here was this white American crowd exalting Elvis Presley without any undertones or hints of anything about his real life that would have taken anything away from his revered status. Elvis, like Michael, faced known and widely reported issues. He took pills, over-indulged in liquor, had legal and moral issues, and yet none of that was mentioned in the same breath with the recognition he was now receiving. This same respect of extolling his virtues and not exacerbating his vices was not and is not being accorded Michael Jackson.

And so I learned again from this Detroit Tigers game, that we as blacks and whites, though segregation has vanished, still live in separate worlds. In our world, whites dismissed Michael's greatness, and even their own principle of innocent till proven guilty was based on their contrived opinion of him and fictitious rumors. Yet in their own world Richard Nixon violated the Constitution but yet was still a great president. J. Edgar Hoover, considered to be the greatest law enforcement executive this country has ever known, broke the law and wire-tapped Martin L. King, Jr.; and Bill Clinton is still considered great even though he was impeached.

So here's my word on Michael. Michael Jackson, regardless of Congressman Peter King's claim, is and will always be the greatest musical talent who ever wrote or sang a song on this earth, and has impacted every country, every culture, and every people on this earth.

CHAPTER 62

"Too Much of Us"

*"But we have this treasure in earthen vessels, that
the excellency of the power may be of God, and not
of us"* **(2 Corinthians 4:7).**

OVER THE LAST thirty plus years I have received many revelations, none quite as important as this one though. Sometimes we are so self-consumed that we simply get in God's way. We are so busy, so important, so focused on our needs and our agenda, and so full of ourselves that people trip over us trying to find Jesus.

Yes, we need God to move, to move our mountains, to move our misery, to move our mountain of bills, to move our enemies, and to move the mess we've made. But maybe what we really need as a church is for the Lord to move us--move us to help others, move us to get out of self, and move us completely out of the way so that those seeking Jesus can find him.

Tell the truth. Most of the time when you hear people talking negatively about their experiences at church it never has anything to do with Jesus or God. It most always has something to do with what someone in the pews or pulpit said, did, didn't do, or shouldn't have said. And what I am suggesting is that if there were less of us, less of our unconverted selves, less of our godless selves still in these earthen vessels we would be less likely to obscure the face and presence of Jesus Christ.

All of us, besides those who stand at our sanctuary doors, are nothing more than ushers in the House of the Lord. We are here to direct others to God and Jesus and not to steer them toward more human confusion and condemnation. We are ushers here to deflect any attention from us toward the one who is able to keep us from falling.

Simply put, when we get in the way and there is too much of us, God's revelation and Jesus manifestation is eclipsed by self-glorification. We need to stop allowing ourselves to be the main focus and for us to, through our conduct, conversation, and character, point our fellow pilgrim to the one who makes wrong right and takes a little and makes it much.

CHAPTER 63

"One Day At A Time"

"Take therefore no thought for tomorrow; for the morrow shall take thought for the things of itself. Sufficient unto the day is the evil thereof."
(Matthew 6:34)

NO MATTER WHO we are, how much we have or do not have, and what life has been like before today - today is really all we have; and even when we try to capture it, it has escape. To see this new day means that God has blessed me again to avoid and overcome the innumerable destructive and life-altering and ending occurrences that are now common.

Therefore, God expects my stewardship to be focused on doing better today not trying to get right tomorrow. This day, Lord, help me to use to discover and do your perfect will and to fulfill your purpose for my life.

One day at a time, that's all we've been given. And perhaps the next day, if granted by God, will be given based on what we did for him and for others the day before. A day has the potential for a lot to be done.

In one day we can:

    a.   Decide to live differently

    b.   Give our life to Jesus Christ

    c.   Make amends for wrongs we've done

    d.   Reconcile ourselves with our church family

    e.   Speak a kind word to someone trying to make it over

    f.   Smile at someone who is frowning at you.

What will you do TODAY to make your life serve a greater purpose and to build His church. Whatever you do, make sure that it is something that will give God a good reason to bless you with another day.

CHAPTER **64**

"When Is Then?"

> *"...and then began man calling*
> *on the name of the Lord"* (Genesis 4:26).

THERE IS PLENTY of precedence, in both our past and our present, where the tripling of trouble, the preponderance of problems, and a crescendo of calamitous circumstance have gotten us to a point along our pilgrimage where our burdens become unbearable. And correspondingly, there is ample biblical evidence that when anything like this occurs this is when it's time to turn to the Lord.

In Genesis 4:26, we are told that after a series of successive sorrowful, sad, and sinful situations that God was merciful to Eve in the death of her son, Abel, by replacing him with Seth. However, before this occurred, a ton of terror, trial, and tribulation had already transpired. Adam and Eve had already faced expulsion and eviction from eternity in paradise; mankind had already traded a treat for a trail, blessings for burdens, a leisure life for a life of labor; and murder had traded places with life.

Well, for me all of this begs the question. At what point does our 'when' become our 'then.' The text tells us that when humans had fallen and when Adam and Eve experienced pain - then man began to call on God. So the question is "when is then?" When are we going to begin to call on the one who is able to minimize mess and maximize mercy? When are we going to call on the one who no matter what has preceded our contact with him can change everything--even wrong into right?

At what point have we had enough of trying to deal with it by ourselves? At what point are we disgusted with living beneath the promises of God? From this text we get the answer. Whenever we have had enough! When we can't stand another lie; when we can't tolerate another fix; and, when we can't stomach anymore sin. That's when we, like Adam and Eve, realize the drastic difference between what we lost and what we had, and our need to call on the Lord.

And it is when we call on the Lord that he gives us life even in death. Even though Adam and Eve had lost Abel, they decided to yield to God, to acknowledge God, and more specifically, to call on the name of God, and God replaced Abel with Seth.

I dare you to decide to look to God. I double dare you to when - whatever it is - let that be your then – and let that THEN be the moment you began to call on the name of the Lord.

CHAPTER 65

Words From Pastor Sheffield
"Tis The Season To Be........."

I DON'T KNOW about you, but I've discovered that for me the older I get the harder it is, at times, to be happy during the holidays. It's hard to be happy during the holidays because of some of the unreasonable expectations that others sometimes place on us to buy this, to go here, to do this, to forget that, to remember this, and to extend and expend to others--even if they are absolutely undeserving--regardless of what it will cost and how long it will take for us to personally recover.

It's hard to be happy during the holidays because quite frankly this time of the year, more than any other, reminds me of all of my losses. This time of year, because our family always gathered together and shared the holidays, inevitably causes me to painfully personally miss my cheerleading mother, Mary Kathryn, my ever-supporting father, Horace, Jr., my compassionate grandfather, Horace, Sr., my godly grandmother, Georgia, and countless helpful others who used to give this season such meaning to me who are now no longer physically here to share it at all. I tell you this alone makes these holidays hard to handle.

It's hard to be happy that time of year when you have to work so hard and long to make the season a festive fellowship. Christmas, my December birthday, and New Year's Eve and New Year's Day, are all delightful yet terribly taxing, and especially so if you invite and allow others to invade your intimate space on these days. Just think of how much fun it will be having to listen to all of those comments you'd wish others would just keep to themselves, enduring discussions about painful and embarrassing events from your past, and having to be around folks who drink too much, play too much, talk too much, and who for the moment at least, act like your home is their castle.

It's hard to be happy during these holidays for all of the reasons stated above and many more. It's even harder than all of this if we lose sight of the real reason for this holiday season. As we spend our money shopping, let us first spend time with Him (Jesus) and continue to prepare ourselves to spend eternity with our Redeemer. As we share ourselves and our gifts with others, let us also take time to share all that we are, all that we have, and all that we've been given with God who is, has been, and will always be our provider. I don't know about you, but with Jesus in my life suddenly it's not so hard to be happy during these holidays.

CHAPTER **66**

"Five Foci for the Faithful"

"....and upon this rock I will build my church; and
the gates of hell shall not prevail against it."
(Matthew 16:18)

THERE ARE SO many interests and issues that can, and often do, consume our affection, our attention, and our time in the church that we sometimes lose sight of why we're here. However, no matter what we do, and from what ministry station we do it, I believe that there are some priorities or specific spiritual tasks that all of us, including the church, must remain committed to. I call these cardinal tasks, ministry undertakings, or the Five Foci of the Faithful.

The Five Foci of the Faithful are:**(1) Personal Piety; (2) Care of the Soul; (3) Social and Community Justice ; (4) Corporate Considerations; and, (5) Church Maintenance.** In this section of the book, I'd like to take some time to explain and unpack each of these foci - or that is, what New Galilee as a whole and each of us as believers should concern ourselves with and be committed to as believers. Let me also say, before I treat Personal Piety, that every deacon, trustee, ministry Leader, and member of New Galilee should pay careful and close attention to these that we might all become more Christ-like - and do more of what Christ did.

CARE OF THE SOUL

The second focus of the faithful is a concentration on the care of the soul, and the care of souls. The care of souls concentrates solely on the well-being of individuals, the members who make us this body. This care goes beyond comforting the grieving, visiting the sick, and counseling the burdened; its goal is the sharing and achievement of the renewal of life and spirit in and through the imposition of the presence of Christ. Toward this, the purposes of the care of the soul are:

1. The giving of comfort that guides and ushers others into a comforting encounter with Jesus Christ.

2. To grow through the interaction with others in the fellowship of Jesus Christ, in ministry, worship, and other times of gathering and redirecting our lives.

3. To concern ourselves with ways of assisting others to be healed, sustained, and reconciled as they face changes, circumstances, and challenges caused by various experiences of life.

CHAPTER 67

"The 3 C's of CHURCH SUCCESS - Acts 2:41-43"

"Then they that gladly received his word were baptized: and the same day there were added unto them about three thousands souls..." (Acts 2:41).

PASTORS, MINISTRIES, AND church leaders around the world pray and search for a way to make their churches grow and succeed. Often, in this quest to be bigger and better, those who search for formulas to grow their churches simply observe others and attempt to do what they have done. While every church and its ministry is different I believe that there are three (3) core cornerstones that must be embraced and practiced for a church to be successful. Those three core cornerstones are seeking, surrendering, and serving.

(1) SEEKING (Acts 2:41). "Then they that gladly received (GK., *dechomai*, to receive by deliberate and ready reception what is offered) were baptized." For our church to succeed we need to be full of believers who faithfully search and seek for God and then without reluctance receive and follow him. And our search for him should be as relentless and persistent as a thirsty man needing water to survive in a dry desert.

(2) *SURRENDER* (Acts 2:42). "And they continued (GK. ***dia pantos***, the period and time frame throughout which something is done) steadfastly in the Apostle's doctrine and fellowship...For too many seekers our search ends once the trouble and trials cease, or until we gain the minimum from the master. Discipleship, or following Jesus, is not a short term preoccupation, it is a lifelong all-consuming occupation. If we are to succeed in ministry we must continue steadfast in our coming, our giving, and in our serving.

(3) *SERVING* (Acts 2:43). "And fear came upon every soul: and many wonders and signs (GK., ***semeion***, that which distinguishes one person from others) were done by the Apostles." We seek and we surrender but for one reason, to seek God and to serve His church. So many come in here in emergency status, in dire despair, and in great financial and social need and our seeking and serving last only until we are rescued or find relief. God is looking for people who feel a debt of gratitude and a commitment to serve God that will last a lifetime and will persist though plagued and problematic.

There are 3 S's of success, and embracing these will achieve sustained church growth.

CHAPTER 68

"Here To Help You!"

"Therefore I endure all things for the elects' sakes, that they may also obtain the salvation which is in Christ Jesus...." (II Timothy 2:10)

EVERY CIRCUMSTANCE, TO determine its real value, must be taken in its complete and overall context. Likewise, some experiences, left to stand alone, may on their face seem adverse, detrimental, and even potentially destructive and harmful. However, if we were to connect our circumstances, join our experiences, and weigh everything that happens to us in the light of some grander, good, and eternal purpose, then what may have initially seemed hurtful may actually end up being helpful.

Paul, in this familiar passage, provides us with a particular perspective that, as saints who seek to serve a divine purpose within a social context (the church), we should seek to enhance and to employ. Paul says, "I endure all things for the elects' sake," which means that in church we should not think solely of ourselves but rather think of how what we are forced to face in the fellowship serves some greater purpose also in those who witness our perseverance. Consequently, I am prepared to endure pain if it results in someone else prospering, ready to endure ridicule if it results in someone else's redemption, set to deal with hardship if it helps others see and gain heaven, and willingly to submit to suffering if it ultimately means that someone else will be saved. Our problem today in the church is that too many are here only for comfort, gain, and personal progress and will not sacrifice anything to see someone else gain.

All of us should be like Paul, prepared "to endure all things if it means someone else will be blessed from my buffeting." I am not here for me. I do not come week after week blind to the plight of others, and so self-absorbed that what affects others has no affect on me. I come to church every week prepared to suffer, ready to be rejected, set to be slain by others, primed for persecution, and expecting to endure hardship willingly if in the end someone besides me can experience what I have enjoyed and share the salvation I have been so freely given.

At New Galilee, we, like Paul, must prayerfully prepare ourselves to "endure all things" if it means others will be blessed and saved as a result. I will gladly go through any trial if it results in someone else's transformation. How about you?

CHAPTER 69

"Prayer's New Destiny"

1. For me as pastor and priest to be free from anything and everything that would resemble or reflect any form of unrighteousness or would be the cause of any offense.

2. For the Lord to make our God-given purpose and mandate to precede us and to perpetually prevail in this new work and in this new place **(Isaiah 43:10-11)**. *Help us to know who we are and what we are supposed to be doing (Isaiah 58).*

3. For the Lord to prepare us, the founders and those whom he sends, with the proper godly perspectives, attitudes, mindsets, and hearts for dedicated and unswerving service in this new work and in this new place.

4. For the Lord to reveal to us the redemptive rudiments of this new work, and how and what he wants us to do for Him that will result in this new work in a new place actually rescuing, saving, and building up the people of His hand that he will be sending us.

5. For the Lord, in this new work in a new place, will prepare its ground to be fertile, fruitful, free of antagonisms - aughts- and strongholds, and to openly work with us so that we always remain open to

His guidance, to His will, and to His purpose so that New Destiny will be all about Jesus and not about us.

OPEN TO GROWTH, Receptive of All, Zealous to Serve, and Governed by Grace, Mercy, and Love.

6. FOR TO now reveal to us and enable us to know those that He has purposed to draw and set in this new work in a new place for the work of the ministry, the equipping of the saints, and for the ex-altation of Jesus' name. **Make us Fishers of Men and of Souls. And, finally, Lord, this is Your Work and Your Church, and we need to hear YOUR Voice and to obey it.}**

CHAPTER **70**

"Expecting the Unexpected"

"He is not here: for he has risen, as he said"
(KJV, Matthew 28:6).

THE PLANNED DEMISE and apparently inevitable outcome of the efforts of those to permanently do away with Jesus completely failed. 'He is not here' is the one statement that is our "stone of hope" hewn out of the "mountain of despair."

All that had occurred and was witnessed all week long since Jesus' triumphant entry to his trumped up trial appeared to only lead to one inevitable and tragic end: Jesus' death. From the facts alone it seemed as if Jesus' fate had been forever sealed. Judging from the deeds of His executioners, and by those who rolled an immovable stone in front of His tomb, any hopes of Jesus being the Savior were now buried in the grave with Him.

The problem is that this pre-resurrection narrative only accounts for the natural occurrences. It does so because the two entities, or those parties who were responsible for Jesus' death, the Jews and Romans, were accustomed to believing that they were unbeatable forces. But they were wrong because they did not expect the unexpected nor did they understand that with GOD ALL things are ALWAYS possible. And this is so even after the fact, after the case has been closed, or the verdict rendered.

People always expect that their treacherous mistreatment and deceitful death blows will prevail. That's because they think that all they are dealing with is us and what we can or cannot do. They do not expect someone with greater power to intervene or to come to our rescue. The message of Easter is that, no matter how it looks now, always expect the unexpected because with God ALL THINGS ARE ALWAYS POSSIBLE.....Just ask Jesus, He Got UP!

CHAPTER 71

New Ways For My New Year

"But seek ye first the kingdom of God"
(Matthew 6:33).

RECENTLY, AS I prepared for the New Year, I took time to write in my journal to the Lord about acquiring some **New Ways for the New Year**. Here is some of my entry on that subject from my personal journal.

"Lord, as I begin this New Year I also begin anew and again. Toward that end as I pray it is clear, there is one thing that I want above all else this year--for me to be completely yours.

Most, if not all of my life, I have done what I wanted. And it has been me pleasing and feeding my flesh that landed me in this pit. So for the coming year, here's what I ask your Holy Spirit to help me to submit to and surrender to:

1. To overcome all of my financial burdens and to work toward achieving the abundant life.

2. To treat and carry myself emotionally, mentally, physically,

legally, psychologically, sexually, and spiritually like the temple I am.

3. To wait in you before I do anything. Anything, even simple things

4. To overcome every hindrance whether self-imposed or from others

5. To love myself, my children, my enemies, and all you have for me

6. To use every God-given gift I have to its fullest

7. To faithfully fulfill my calling and to live out my godly purpose

CHAPTER **72**

"A Recent Revelation"

I NOW KNOW that every day I must recommit and resubmit my life to Jesus Christ. As certain as I am that I am saved, I am more certain that we are challenged daily to be more devoted to Christ than the day before.

I say that because when we defeat the devil on Wednesday, and win, we can be assured that his devices, trials, and temptations will be even more troubling on Thursday. The devil will not leave us alone no matter how resolute we are. He is determined to undermine God's purpose in our lives and to detour the Lord's direction for our families, our service, and our ministries.

The problem is that we are too passive in the face of assaults, antagonisms, and in that all-out war the enemy rages against us. We have to be more fierce and bold, and more confrontational than the enemy. We must be MORE than the devil; more prayerful than he is painful; more committed than he is confusing; and more powerful than he is alluring.

Before we can advance the Lord's cause, build His church and His ministry, and live and enjoy the abundant life, we have to win this wrestling match. We must so confound, suppress, and defeat the devil through prayer, spiritual disciplines, assembling together, and by seeking the Spirit of God that he concedes before he proceeds. We should be so anointed that when the devil seeks to destroy our marriages, our homes, our finances, and our ministries that he is immediately disappointed because we have already declared them, through the blood of Jesus, OFF LIMITS!

I'm putting the devil where he belongs: out of my life, out of my way, out of my family, out of New Destiny and am putting him back in his pit!

CHAPTER 73

"No Less Than God"

By Rev. Horace L. Sheffield, III

"...for He makes His sun rise on the evil and on the good, and sends rain on the just and on the unjust"
(Matthew 5:45b).

ISN'T IT AMAZING how we profess to be Christ-like, which is in essence to be like God, and yet we act so ungodly. How is it that we expect God to extend this matchless mercy toward us in our mistakes when we withdraw the same toward others in their shortcomings?

How do we dare decide who should experience the grace of God and be allowed into His presence? If the truth be told, based on our behavior, we should be banned from even mentioning his name. What am I trying to say? I am suggesting that in our conduct, in our character, and in our conversation, if we profess to love God and to be acquiring Christ-likeness - we should treat others no less than God does!

How does God treat others? Well, this text tells us that he is indiscriminate. He doesn't only provide for the good but he makes allowances for the evil as well. Hedoes make certain that the just are sustained - he ensures that the same rain nourishes the unjust. Now, if God goes out of his way to treat all he has created with mercy, why are we so quick to treat miserably those who live differently, believe differently, and who have made different choices than us.

Beloved, when it comes to others, rich or poor, black or white, straight or gay, we should treat people no less than God treats them. We should treat them no less than God treats us, and respond to them just as God, who knows all about us, responds to us.

Even more, we are called to likewise love them as God loves them. We should try to reach this point and place in our pilgrimage in which the only thing that we see when we look at others are God's cherished children. If God makes certain that he is inclusive of everyone in His care regardless of our proclivities, predicaments, and problems, we should do no less than God, and be mindful of others without respect to their faults, failings, or frailties?

Whatever we say, whatever we do, and however we treat each other, it should be no less than what God is and does with us.

CHAPTER **74**

What Kind Of Light Are You?

(Matthew 5:16)

DARKNESS IS EVERYWHERE. It's in our world. It has come to be a mark on us as a people and to disturb our nation. It is common with our communities, and most often seen, even at times within our churches, in how we interact with one another. Given the weight, weariness, and worries of this inescapable darkness sometimes when we come to church, after having wrestled with all of this and more, we need to be able to lighten things up by just having a good laugh.

Sometimes we are just too serious. We are just unable to simply enjoy ourselves. We are so preoccupied with our predicaments that we don't permit others or ourselves to have fun with ourselves, with God, and with one another. Therefore some Sundays we need to provide some holy humor for the pews from the pulpit.

That's what I'd like to do. Of course, when Christmas season comes around each year, bright lights twinkle everywhere we look. I would like to ask you, "What kind of light are you"?

Here are some to choose from. Are you a:

TRAFFIC LIGHT: Always trying to direct everything and never doing anything yourself, but always trying to direct where you go and what you do.

GREEN LIGHT: Will go for anything, never questions the cause, never challenges the character – JUST goes along to get along.

RED LIGHT: Always putting a road block in the way – *Obnoxious Obstructionist* – As one person they can find more reasons against it than the whole church can find in favor of it – **Won't Do – and Won't Let You DO!**

SPOT LIGHT: Always able to point out your faults – to show others Your shortcomings – can see everything well except themselves.

NEON LIGHT: Looks good on the outside – but dangerous when disturbed - pretty but painful – See one thing – experience something different – **BETTER LEFT ALONE.**

PORCH LIGHT: Only comes on when company comes over – Only shines on Sunday – during service – IF EVEN THEN.

TIMED LIGHTS: Only flashes based on who is or who is not preaching – singing – or praying. Turns off as quick as it turns on.

STRING LIGHTS: If one is out – None will turn ON. And you have to examine one to try to find out which one it is that is keeping the others from coming on.

STREET LIGHT: Only turns on when it DARK .

PILOT LIGHT: Unseen – but lights the fire – *Sets the Church on fire.*

NIGHT LIGHT: Helps those in darkness to see their *Way OUT* – See their *Way UP* – See their *Way In* – and see their *way THROUGH.*

SEARCH LIGHT: Trying to seek and save the lost – *Shines their light in darkness* – so they can see the lifeline.

CHAPTER 75

Vision For My Pastoral Ministry

HAVING BEEN AT New Destiny for a while now, I thought it appropriate to once again re-visit and to restate some fundamental things that define my vision of my pastoral ministry. Below, as I share my thoughts on this subject I ask for your response and personal interaction as you read and reflect upon each of them. My vision for the mission of pastoral ministry at New Destiny is as follows.

1. TO BE Biblically-Based: The Bible serves as the sacrosanct (highest and untouchable) and supreme standard by which we evaluate all practices, policy, beliefs, and behavior in the Body of Christ (II Timothy 3:16). We cannot become a Christ-like people or congregation without studying the WORD.

2. DESIRED LEADERSHIP Qualifications: To search for and to only install leaders who have demonstrated a visible ability, who have been stewards, and have displayed at all times consistent Christian character (I Timothy 3:1-13 and Exodus 18:21). We seek congregational and ministry leaders who will strive for quality of Christian concern and service and whose conduct will affirm our witness and will not take away from our message.

3. COMMITMENT TO A Spiritual Standard: Do all that we do to the glory of God, and not the pleasing of men. Stay in constant contact with the Lord and Savior Jesus Christ that it may never be said of us that we have left our first love (Jesus) (Revelations 2:4) Maintain a perpetual pattern of Christian behavior which sets us apart as the Lord's people from others, whether in the church or in the world (I Peter 1:14-15). Always place our trust in the Lord and strive to do that which is right.

4. DISPLAY COMPASSIONATE Concern to Those We Serve and Who are in our charge: Provide the type of prompt, personal, and affectionate attention that we ourselves would also hope to receive. Display no bias of service or differentiation of response toward those who are in our charge.

CHAPTER 76

Doing Our Best

IT IS RECORDED that Jesus said, *"No man having put his hands to the plough, and looking back, is fit for the kingdom of God."* Beloved, this text clearly and emphatically tells that we have been given a task by Jesus and that we are responsible to perform it without excuse.

I cannot speak for you but I am clearly at a point in my life where I live each day and do my best to prove to my Lord that the love I have for him can be proven by more than just words. I'm at a point in which mere effort alone in serving him and his church is insufficient. It is time, with whatever years I have remaining, to do my very best to serve him and his church completely, without reservation, and without excuse. Brothers and sisters of New Destiny it is time for us to do our best to build a vibrant bustling ministry that reflects the needs of this challenging era.

And we cannot do that if we give Christ and his church anything other than our very best. He, God that is, gave us his very best when he gave us his Son, Jesus the Christ. And if he had not, we would not have escaped hell. We would not have made it through trial and tribulation, and survived all that we have endured. So here is where I am. I am issuing a challenge to everyone here to look at yourselves and make a commitment to do our best to build up this ministry by spreading the Good News of the Gospel, by our benevolent and merciful acts toward others, and most importantly, by our making a firm commitment to building some ministry in New Destiny.

Let me help you with that. A few months ago we held a planning meeting focused on what we were doing right in our ministry and how we needed to improve our efforts. So, if you are sitting here this morning wondering what you can do to achieve your very best to build New Destiny, here, let me help you.

Here's what you can do: choose to be kind and courteous; find out what people you share your pew with are going through and decide to help them through it; come to church every week with a spirit of thanksgiving and share the same with others; be determined to not let anyone say anything to you that would dissuade your service or discourage your dedication to the work of the ministry; make a habit of praying about the things that bother you before you say anything about it to others; likewise, make a habit of praying for people that bother you or have done wrong to you before you say or do anything about it; plan and commit to spend time with God daily to consecrate yourself to the work of the ministry; and regularly resolve that no matter what and no matter who, that each day you are going to be more like Jesus than you were the day before.

CHAPTER 77

Some Things The Lord Told Me

I AM ALWAYS interested in hearing from the Lord. In fact, in the Old Testament the people of God were always positioning themselves to hear the voice of God (quof Yahweh). And they listened for His voice because they depended upon the instruction and life that was contained in His voice. This is why the people of old would ask, "Is there a Word from the Lord" (debar adonai)?

Consequently as this current year ends and a new one begins to dawn, here are a few of my recent meditations and purposed prayers I was given that I wanted to share with you. What are some of yours?

Here are some of mine:

WHAT THE LORD TOLD ME
You need the certainty of my loving presence in order to weather the storms of life.

HERE'S WHAT I TOLD THE LORD
If you sustained me in my wilderness my faith now tells me that you can provide for me in your promised land.

FOR THE MINISTRY

Organize, galvanize, concretize, and then help us to realize your vision and our purpose.

AND MY PRAYERS
Lord, purge my carnality that competes with my spirituality.

Lord, please provide instruction and correction for my direction and show me what to do and where to go.

Lord, set me free from all remaining encumbrances and bless me to prosper mightily.

Lord, show me how to grow this ministry and reveal to me what is our unique work of the ministry.

"It's People Like You Who Show They Care"

(A Special Tribute to My Dear Friend
& Brother in Christ, Rev. Horace L. Sheffield, III)

It's people like you, who show they care
They give to others and always share
Reaching out to the many lost souls
Standing firm on the belief they hold

You make this world a better place
Adding Beauty to this Human Race
God definitely has his hands on you
For the many wonderful things you do

I feel so very blessed to see
The wonderful person you came to be
Helping Others, You're gentle and kind
No better Friend can I ever find

May God continue to bless your life
As you work with the many problems and strife
My Spiritual Brother from deep within,
Thank You, Horace, for being my Friend!

By Mary L. Parker

Mary Parker and I worked together at the Southeast Michigan Council of governments while I was in my junior and senior year of college. We shared many things together like dreams and disappointments. But the most important thing that we shared was our love for the Lord

Jesus Christ. Of all the people I have worked with, Mary Parker is the only one who took time to say her thank you to me in the form of a poem. It is for that reason that I include it within this book for truly it was when written, and continues to be for me, "a good word for a better life." Thanks, Mary, for showing me how you cared.

CHAPTER 78

The Best Way
To Celebrate Christmas

DEAR MEMBER OF New Destiny and the Body of Christ,

As we get busy preparing to celebrate the designated birth of Christ, or Christmas, by making our gift lists, planning our family meals, and searching to find appropriate ways to say thank you and to express our love to those who we loved and who have shown love to us this year, let us consider a few things. I suggest you add to that list.

Give more of yourself to God, in Jesus Christ, as you end this year and prepare to begin a new one. There have been many reasons, some legitimate and understandable, as to why we failed to serve better, to devote more of ourselves to Jesus, and to faithfully fulfill our obligations and pledges to the church. All of what we did not do is behind us. Let us stop right now and say to ourselves, and mean it "Lord, I promise that I will give more to Jesus and to His church next year than I did last year."

Give more of yourself to the Church of Jesus Christ. Lyle Schaller, a modern church demographer, recently said that "for the first time in the history of Christianity in North America there are more believers than belongers." When asked why this was, he responded "because people say that they and God are fine. It's the rest of the people they have problems with." I understand how challenging the church has been and can be. Often our ministries are full of people who love Jesus so much but can't stand anyone else. Nonetheless, Christ died for His church and loves His church, and he has called us to serve His church as I. J. Van Ness has said "regardless of others."

Give the gift of our witness and other's salvation. The best way for us to say thank you to Jesus is by committing ourselves to the same work, same purpose, and same priority with which Jesus' whole life and ministry concerned itself. Jesus, according to Mark 2, came to seek and to save the lost. If we are here to follow Him, then we need to be as zealous in reaching the lost at all cost even as He was. Surely, God isn't asking us to die for that to happen. No, he just wants us to share the new life we have come to know in Jesus to all that we know and with all whom we meet. Let us lift Jesus up in all that we do and with all that we say, and HE WILL draw all men, all sinners, and all who are dead to new life in Him.